דרור יקרא
The Call of Freedom

Rabbi Karen Gluckstern–Reiss
Edited by Karen L. Stein

The United Synagogue of Conservative Judaism
Department of Youth Activities

UNITED SYNAGOGUE OF CONSERVATIVE JUDAISM

DEPARTMENT OF YOUTH ACTIVITIES

Jules A. Gutin	DIRECTOR
Gila Hadani Ward	ASSISTANT DIRECTOR
Karen L. Stein	EDUCATION COORDINATOR
Aharon Charnov	PUBLICATIONS COORDINATOR
Janine Abbate	PROJECTS COORDINATOR
Ezra Androphy	ACTIVITIES COORDINATOR
Shana Sisk	USY 50TH ANNIVERSARY COORDINATOR
Yossi Garr	CENTRAL SHALIACH
Yitzchak Jacobsen	DIRECTOR, ISRAEL OFFICE
David Keren	DIRECTOR, ISRAEL PROGRAMS

NATIONAL YOUTH COMMISSION

Marshall Baltuch, CO-CHAIR
Dr. Marilyn Lishnoff Wind, CO-CHAIR

UNITED SYNAGOGUE OF CONSERVATIVE JUDAISM

Stephen S. Wolnek, PRESIDENT
Rabbi Jerome M. Epstein, EXECUTIVE VICE-PRESIDENT

A publication of the National Youth Commission
United Synagogue of Conservative Judaism
155 Fifth Avenue, New York, New York 10010
http://www.uscj.org/usy

First Edition, 2000

Printed and bound in the United States of America by Phoenix Color Corp.
Cover design by Aharon Charnov
Production, layout and design by Karen L. Stein

CONTENTS

EDITOR'S PREFACE

On a recent trip to Boston, I noted the quotation from a monument just outside the Holocaust Memorial. "Pause here to reflect on the consequence of a world in which there is no freedom—a world in which basic human rights are not protected." This concept was written so simply, yet had a resounding effect.

Dror Yikra—The Call of Freedom is more than a theoretical discussion about freedom. It is designed to cause us to stop and reflect upon a world in which there is no freedom and discover the close connection the Jewish people have had with the concept and quest for freedom. The inspiration for this book came easily: as a celebration of USY's 50th Anniversary, it seemed logical to discuss the importance of Yovel—the 50th Jubilee year in Biblical history and the Convention's Boston location easily helped us mark our Freedom Trail.

We are fortunate that Rabbi Karen Gluckstern-Reiss has accepted our invitation to author this innovative text. A talented educator and scholar, Rabbi Gluckstern-Reiss brought ideas to life and has allowed classical Jewish sources to speak to modern considerations. It has been a privilege to work with her throughout the creation of this book and to bring to light our definitions of freedom together.

This text has been enriched by those who have read the original manuscripts and who played a crucial role in shaping this book: Rabbi Jerome M. Epstein, Jonathan Greenberg, Jack Gruenberg, Jules Gutin, and Gila Hadani Ward. This completed edition also benefited greatly from the contributions of David Srebnik who took great measures to help shape the interactive educational components of the book.

As you read this book, you will notice a cast of friendly characters—"*Screen Beans* ©" For the most part, these icons were not chosen at random, but rather are there to help guide you through the text. True freedom can only be achieved if you first free your imagination.

I am grateful to my colleagues in the Youth Department of the United Synagogue of Conservative Judaism who have all been extremely encouraging and insightful throughout the entire process. Additionally, I must thank Ari Goldberg who has continued to be a source of support and guidance and whose shoes I still strive to fill.

Karen L. Stein
December, 2000

PREFACE

"Ben Zoma taught: Who is wise? One who learns from all persons... who is mighty? One who conquers his evil impulse... Who is rich? One who is happy with his portion... Who is honored? One who honors his fellows." I would add, "Who is free? One who strives towards freedom for all humans."

The core values that underscore freedom are central to our Jewish experience. We live in a world where the struggle for freedom has been a centerpiece of the last two centuries for a multitude of nations and peoples.

Our singularly unique way of experiencing freedom within the framework of *halakha* charges us as Conservative Jews to make freedom a sacred state of being. Guaranteeing freedom is an act of sanctity, a component of *tikkun olam*. This book serves as one venue to hear the call of freedom as it manifests itself in our communities.

It is my hope that we each find inspiration in this book to struggle for the freedom of others, understanding that it is only when another is freed that we can each experience true freedom. I learned this lesson from two dear individuals; my father, Phil Reiss, who taught me from an early age that freedom means doing the right thing, even if it is not the most popular thing, and my aunt, Maralyn Itzkowitz, who encouraged me to have a passion for the ongoing battle for freedom even when others just don't 'get it'. Their lessons have inspired me throughout life, and throughout the writing of this book.

I want to thank Ms. Karen Stein for her ongoing contributions in editing and publication of this book. Her skills and talents helped guide and shape this book as its form emerged. Thanks as well to two dear friends, Rabbi Lisa Gelber and Rabbi Francine Roston who served as wonderful listening boards as the book hit rough spots on its road to being. A special thank you to all my friends and family for their understanding as this book consumed my freedom and came into being.

The act of one individual can be extremely powerful. May you be a Jew who in your actions brings freedom to the most important race in the world -the human race.

Rabbi Karen Gluckstern-Reiss
Heshvan 5761

TO THE READER...

Throughout this book, there are essentially five key educational components.

1. **Text and Questions**— Each topic discussed within the book has a number of primary and secondary references (quotes) as well as the author's narration. Additionally, the guiding questions will help lead you through the narrative so that you can work either with or without a facilitator.

2. **Exercises**—Each unit has a series of personal exercises that will allow you to further delve into the subject and should help shape your personal definition of freedom as well as think about what role freedom plays in your life. These exercises are all marked with a friendly "screen bean" doing his stretches!

3. **Think About This**— Dilemmas and "what if's" that allow you to "Think About" what you would do if your freedom was compromised. Each of these short situations are signified by a "screen bean" with a good idea!

4. **A Call to Action**— "In the News" pieces that either highlight the accomplishments of an individual or group in promoting greater freedom or an information piece that will further your knowledge about a current event issue directly related to the freedom discussed in the chapter.

5. **Reflections**— These boxes which are found at the end of a section will give you an opportunity to stop along the way and think about the freedom you just learned about.

FREEDOM—AN INTRODUCTION

This sourcebook, *Dror Yikra: The Call of Freedom* challenges each of us both as Jews and as citizens of the modern world. It askes the basic philosophical questions about freedom, where it comes from, and how it is granted. It puts forth the charge of the responsibility for safeguarding and promoting the institutions of freedom. The book explores the tension between guaranteeing freedom and living as an observant Jew.

The sources in this sourcebook

There are three sources that are utilized in this sourcebook. The primary and central sources examined are those from our traditional Jewish text. These sources represent the richly woven fabric of our tradition. Often these texts may not appear to directly relate to the theme of freedom. There will be times when it will be necessary to use allegory, generalizations or study aids to understand how a text can help shed light on our understanding of freedom. There will be other times when the text stands alone in inspiring our struggle towards freedom for all. A second form of primary Jewish sources that will be examined in this book are statements published in this generation by the Conservative movement. These statements will be presented as a way of understanding the direction leaders of our movement have taken on a particular issue. Though these sources do not always quote the primary Jewish text that inspired our leaders to call us to action, they are rich in inspiration to change. The third group of sources that can be found throughout the book are not Jewish, but are quotes of individuals of this past generation, who through their involvement in public light continue to inspire us to call out for freedom for all people of the world.

How to use this sourcebook

There are four sections to this book: A Time to Be Free, Freedom: Do You Get It?, Rights and Responsibilities of Freedom, and A Call to Freedom.

The section on Jewish time examines moments of the Jewish calendar that relate to freedom. *Pesach*, *Shabbat* and the *Yovel*, each represent a different type of freedom, but together shed light on some Jewish approaches to the idea of freedom.

"Freedom - Do You Get It?" asks the basic philosophical questions about freedom. It explores where our freedom is derived from, if it is innate, or if it is something we acquire. This section also explores the inherent tension between being an observant Jew and a member of a free society at the start of the new century.

"Rights and Responsibilities" considers freedom in light of civil liberties. It examines the safeguarding of both communal and individual freedoms, particularly issues where the two intersect or conflict. This section raises questions about those freedoms that are continuing to evolve, and calls us to get involved in the ongoing pursuit of freedom for all.

This leads to the last section of the book, "A Call to Freedom," a call to action. We are obligated to be a part of efforts for *tikun olam*—building a better world.

Section One: Defining Freedom

Which of these words would you choose to define Freedom?

- License
- Liberty
- Independence
- Permission
- Immunity
- Exemption
- Release
- Discharge
- Probation
- Facility
- Range
- Latitude
- Play Freehand
- Wide berth
- Room

- Emancipation
- Autonomy
- Self-government
- Non-intervention
- Have a will of one's own
- Take leave
- Feel at home
- Permit
- Allow
- Untie
- Loose
- Unchain
- At will
- Uncompelled
- Unbiased

- Rampant
- Wanton
- Irrepressible
- Hand's off
- *Laissez faire*
- Extricate
- Scot-free
- Autonomous
- Ungoverned
- Carefree
- Out of control
- Absolute
- Live and let live
- Unforced
- Redemption

What other words or phrases would you use if you were defining freedom?

_____
_____
_____

Is it possible to categorize these words in any particular way?

_____
_____
_____
_____

Compare and contrast "Freedom" and "Being allowed to do anything you want."

_____
_____
_____

What do you think about the statement: "Freedom is absolute—either you have it or your don't."

_____
_____
_____

According to the definition in the dictionary:

(1)The state of being free of constraints.
(2)Political independence.
(3)Free will.
(4)Frankness or boldness of expression.
(5)Unrestricted access or use.

Compare the dictionary definition with your categories from the previous page.

_____

_____

_____

_____

_____

EXERCISE: Freedom Is....

Mark the appropriate place for each item below:

	Strongly Disagree					Strongly Agree
Freedom is earned	1	2	3	4	5	6
Freedom is a right	1	2	3	4	5	6
There is nothing that any individual cannot attain	1	2	3	4	5	6
Freedom is something that must be limited in order for communities to survive	1	2	3	4	5	6
Freedom is a threat to a religious community	1	2	3	4	5	6
Freedom is a threat to a democratic society	1	2	3	4	5	6
Freedom is never really attainable	1	2	3	4	5	6
Freedom is something that you are born with	1	2	3	4	5	6
Total freedom is not good for a community	1	2	3	4	5	6
There is no such thing as total freedom	1	2	3	4	5	6

LOOK TO THE SOURCES

Are these concepts of freedom Jewish ones? When we look at Jewish sources we find that there are three words that define freedom - *heirut, dror,* and *hofesh*. Read through the texts from the Talmud and Tanakh (Hebrew Bible) on the next three pages to see how the different concepts of Freedom are defined.

Hofesh

כִּי תִקְנֶה עֶבֶד עִבְרִי שֵׁשׁ שָׁנִים יַעֲבֹד וּבַשְּׁבִעִת יֵצֵא לַחָפְשִׁי חִנָּם׃

"When you acquire a Hebrew slave, six years he shall work, in the seventh year he shall go free, without payment." (Exodus, 21:2)

כִּי־יִמָּכֵר לְךָ
אָחִיךָ הָעִבְרִי אוֹ הָעִבְרִיָּה וַעֲבָדְךָ שֵׁשׁ שָׁנִים וּבַשָּׁנָה
הַשְּׁבִיעִת תְּשַׁלְּחֶנּוּ חָפְשִׁי מֵעִמָּךְ׃ וְכִי־תְשַׁלְּחֶנּוּ חָפְשִׁי
מֵעִמָּךְ לֹא תְשַׁלְּחֶנּוּ רֵיקָם׃ הַעֲנֵיק תַּעֲנִיק לוֹ מִצֹּאנְךָ
וּמִגָּרְנְךָ וּמִיִּקְבֶךָ אֲשֶׁר בֵּרַכְךָ יְהוָה אֱלֹהֶיךָ תִּתֶּן־לוֹ׃ וְזָכַרְתָּ
כִּי עֶבֶד הָיִיתָ בְּאֶרֶץ מִצְרַיִם וַיִּפְדְּךָ יְהוָה אֱלֹהֶיךָ עַל־כֵּן
אָנֹכִי מְצַוְּךָ אֶת־הַדָּבָר הַזֶּה הַיּוֹם׃

"If a fellow Hebrew, man or woman, is sold to you, he shall serve six years, and in the seventh year you shall set him free. When you set him free do not let him go empty-handed... Bear in mind that you were slaves in the Land of Egypt and the Lord your God redeemed you; therefore I enjoin this commandment upon you today."
(Deuteronomy 15:12-15)

How would you define the type of freedom of *hofesh*?

_____

_____

_____

Based upon these texts, where do you think freedom comes from?

_____

_____

_____

Hofesh is found most often in relation to one who is released from slavery or bondage. These texts are representative of freedom of being. In each source an individual is freed from slavery, or an individual is released from bondage. The freedom comes from the slave owner, but the commandment to free them comes from God. It is a description of liberation.

Dror

It is important to remember that the Biblical text was written without preserving the vocalization. You might understand a word differently depending on the vocalization. An example of how this might be true in English would be the word 'flour', which vocalized differently is 'flower'. Our text here is based on a change in the vocalization of the word 'h.r.t.'; read originally as graven, harut, but the same letters with other vocals means liberty, heirut. By transforming the vocalization the Rabbis are able to expand or limit the understanding of the text.

וְקִדַּשְׁתֶּם אֵת שְׁנַת הַחֲמִשִּׁים שָׁנָה וּקְרָאתֶם
דְּרוֹר בָּאָרֶץ לְכָל־יֹשְׁבֶיהָ יוֹבֵל הִוא תִּהְיֶה לָכֶם וְשַׁבְתֶּם אִישׁ
אֶל־אֲחֻזָּתוֹ וְאִישׁ אֶל־מִשְׁפַּחְתּוֹ תָּשֻׁבוּ׃

"And you shall hallow the fiftieth year. You shall proclaim liberty throughout the land for all its inhabitants. It shall be a jubilee for you: each of you shall return to his holding and each of you shall return to his family."
(Leviticus 25:10)

הַדָּבָר אֲשֶׁר־הָיָה אֶל־יִרְמְיָהוּ מֵאֵת יְהֹוָה אַחֲרֵי כְּרֹת הַמֶּלֶךְ צִדְקִיָּהוּ בְּרִית
אֶת־כָּל־הָעָם אֲשֶׁר בִּירוּשָׁלַםִ לִקְרֹא לָהֶם דְּרוֹר׃ לְשַׁלַּח
אִישׁ אֶת־עַבְדּוֹ וְאִישׁ אֶת־שִׁפְחָתוֹ הָעִבְרִי וְהָעִבְרִיָּה חָפְשִׁים
לְבִלְתִּי עֲבָד־בָּם בִּיהוּדִי אָחִיהוּ אִישׁ׃

"The word came to Jeremiah from the Lord after King Zedakiah had made a covenant with all the people in Jerusalem to proclaim liberty among them, that everyone should set free his Hebrew slaves, both male and female, and that no one should keep his fellow Judean enslaved."
(Jeremiah 34:8-9)

דכולי עלמא דרור לשון
חירות, מאי משמע? - דתניא: אין דרור אלא לשון חירות. אמר רבי
יהודה מה לשון דרור - כמדייר בי דיירא, ומוביל סחורה בכל מדינה.

"*Dror* (liberty) is none other than the language of freedom. Rabbi Yehudah says - what is this language of *dror*? To teach us that *dror* is when a person can live where that person chooses (be *medayer*, from the root phonetic *dror*) and be able to trade in any country."
(Rosh HaShana 9b)

Dar = to dwell, to live; medayer=one who lives there, one who dwells; sounds like dror=freedom

How would you define the type of freedom of *dror*?

_____

_____

_____

Based upon these texts, where do you think freedom comes from?

_____

_____

_____

Dror is all about the time of freedom, or *the call of freedom*. God proclaims freedom at given times in order to sanctify time and space. In this time of freedom, when the call comes, people, land and time all must be freed. This is a physical freedom, but it is also a spiritual freedom. The call comes out from God, based on the promise of the covenant.

Heirut

והלוחות מעשה אלהים המה והמכתב מכתב
אלהים הוא חרות על הלוחות. אל תקרא חרות אלא חרות.
שאין לך בן חורין אלא מי שעוסק בתלמוד תורה.

Rabbi Yehoshua ben Levi taught: it is written: "And the tablets were the work of God, graven (*harut*) upon the tablets." Do not read *harut* (graven) but rather *herut* (freedom), for no person is free except one who engages in the study of Torah.

(*Pirkei Avot* 6:2)

How would you define the type of freedom of *heirut*?

_____

_____

_____

What does it mean that one can only be free if engaging in study of Torah?

_____

_____

_____

Heirut is about the state of liberty. It is a social, political or religious state of being. *Heirut* can be derived from legislation, from social change, or from God.

<u>Putting it Together:</u> Based on these three terms write a definition for the concept 'Jewish Freedom':

_____

_____

_____

TYPES OF FREEDOM

Exploring the universal concepts of freedom, and comparing these to the Jewish concepts of freedom enables us to delineate three general categories of freedom. There is obvious overlap among the categories, however it is possible to relate each of them to the freedom of an individual, communal freedom, and the freedom of a society.

Physical

The concepts of slavery and imprisonment are the obvious examples of physical restraint, leading to the yearning for physical freedom. There are too many cultures and countries in our world that continue to allow slavery of citizens, places where physical freedom is not a right experienced by all individuals. The idea of prison is utilized in all cultures and countries around the world; the theory is that threatening an individual's physical freedom is enough deterrent to limit crime. However, it is also possible to experience such restraint without the extreme situ-

"In the future days, which we seek to make secure, we look forward to a world founded upon four essential human freedoms.

The first is freedom of speech and expression - everywhere in the world.

The second is freedom of every person to worship God in his own way - everywhere in the world.

The third is freedom from want.

The fourth is freedom from fear."

Franklin D. Roosevelt, Address to Congress, January 6, 1941

ation of being an actual slave or in prison. When we are limited in our physical abilities and cannot fully experience the world around us it is possible that we are not experiencing physical freedom. For example, when we enslave ourselves to notions of what a perfect body looks like, or how a perfect face should appear, we are not experiencing physical freedom. When society cannot or will not accommodate our physical limitations, we do not have physical freedom.

What are ways in which a person might be limited in his or her experience of physical freedom?

_____

_____

_____

Who or what are the sources of these limitations?

_____

_____

_____

How can these limitations be overcome?

_____

_____

_____

Political

When an individual is limited in her or his freedom because of governmental legislation, that person will seek out political freedom. This restraint on freedom could derive from a person's political views, or affiliations, from their religious beliefs, from their gender or race. Seeking political freedom can entail civil disobedience, legislative changes as well as educational changes in attitude. Political freedom is not always dependent on a large scale change. It can come from the act of one individual, such as Rosa Parks' refusal to move to the back of the bus.

What are ways in which a person might be limited in their political freedom?

_____

_____

_____

Who or what are the sources of these limitations?

_____

_____

_____

How can these limitations be overcome?

_____

_____

_____

Spiritual

There is a kabbalistic concept called *'yerida lifney ha-aliyah,'* descent before ascent. In order to experience the uplifting of spiritual freedom there needs to be a descent to chaos. When we experience spiritual imprisonment we feel like we are living in a darkened cage. We must believe that life will not always last in this descent, that there will be light after the darkness. That is how we discover our spiritual freedom.

This descent might be a drastic one, rejecting a life of Torah, or a less drastic one, struggling with prayer or God. The tension remains constant, working to move with the challenge in order to get beyond it to freedom. This is an ongoing struggle, one that remains with us throughout our journeys through life. Spiritual freedom is our right and ability to be on this journey unrestricted.

What are ways in which a person might be limited in their spiritual freedom?

_____

_____

_____

Who or what are the sources of these limitations?

_____

_____

_____

How can these limitations be overcome?

_____

_____

_____

FREEDOM TO--FREEDOM FROM--FREEDOM OF

Throughout this book we will explore the many faces of freedom. We will ask if a particular freedom is a freedom to do something, a freedom from a limitation, or a freedom of a certain type. There are many places where it may be difficult to distinguish between the implications of freedom for the individual and for the community. Sometimes freedom for one will result in a deprivation of freedom for another. Freedom from one type of bondage will create lack of freedom to do something for others. You, the reader, will always have to ask how an issue represents a freedom to/ freedom from/ freedom of, whether it protects the individual, the society or both, and how.

EXERCISE:

We The People...

Imagine for a moment that you are writing a constitution for a brand new community, which will guarantee freedom to all its residents.

Write a statement to express this guarantee:

_____
_____
_____
_____
_____
_____
_____
_____
_____
_____
_____
_____
_____
_____

List ways in which freedom of the community is guaranteed through limitations of the freedom of the individual:

_____
_____
_____
_____
_____
_____
_____

List ways in which freedom of the community is limited by guaranteeing the freedom of the individual:

_____
_____
_____
_____
_____
_____

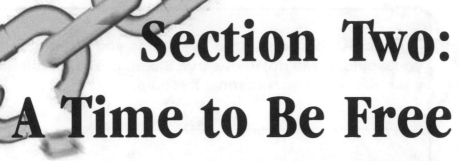

Section Two: A Time to Be Free

A season is set for everything, a time for every experience under heaven.

(Ecclesiastes 3:1)

Time is sacred in Jewish life. We sanctify time with our rituals of daily prayer, our weekly observance of *Shabbat*, our annual observances of holidays. We recognize the movement of the calendar through *Rosh Hodesh*. Within this calendar of time there are moments of Jewish time that illustrate our Jewish connection to freedom.

Shabbat: A Time to be Free

Shabbat is a glorious time of redemption. It is our weekly rest day, a moment when we gather with our loved ones, with our community, and dedicate time and space to God and the Jewish people. We set one day aside to appreciate all the things we are often too busy or occupied to notice during the week. The holiness of the day is predicated on the communal imitation of God's being, of God's rest. *Shabbat* is a liberating day; we are liberated from our daily work, from everyday concerns.

וַיְכַל אֱלֹהִים בַּיּוֹם הַשְּׁבִיעִי מְלַאכְתּוֹ אֲשֶׁר עָשָׂה וַיִּשְׁבֹּת בַּיּוֹם הַשְּׁבִיעִי
מִכָּל־מְלַאכְתּוֹ אֲשֶׁר עָשָׂה. וַיְבָרֶךְ אֱלֹהִים אֶת־יוֹם הַשְּׁבִיעִי
וַיְקַדֵּשׁ אֹתוֹ כִּי בוֹ שָׁבַת מִכָּל־מְלַאכְתּוֹ אֲשֶׁר־בָּרָא אֱלֹהִים לַעֲשׂוֹת.

"And God ceased on the seventh day from all the work that God had done. And God blessed the seventh day and declared it holy, because on it God ceased from all the work of creation...."

(Genesis 2:2-3)

How do we learn from the cessation of God's labor that we too must rest from work on the seventh day?

_____

_____

_____

When we cease from working on Shabbat to observe Shabbat, what freedoms do we have?

_____

_____

_____

EXERCISE: List up to five things you do (or things you think you would like to do) to observe Shabbat. Then, rank them to show your affect on your personal freedom.

	Little effect (I feel very free)				Big effect (I don't feel free)	
1	1	2	3	4	5	6
2	1	2	3	4	5	6
3	1	2	3	4	5	6
4	1	2	3	4	5	6
5	1	2	3	4	5	6

Now, rate those same observances on their importance in preserving the spiritual freedom of Shabbat:

	Most Important				Least Important	
1	1	2	3	4	5	6
2	1	2	3	4	5	6
3	1	2	3	4	5	6
4	1	2	3	4	5	6
5	1	2	3	4	5	6

There are times when this liberation is considered by some to be a burden. The rules and regulations surrounding the observance of *Shabbat* are viewed by some as an intrusion on their desire to relax, to rest, in their own ways, ways that might contradict the *mitzvot* of the day. Attendance at services, the commandment to have three glorious meals, regulations restricting work, writing, and entertainment, can be viewed by those who are not *Shabbat* observers as coercion, as an intrusion on their personal space. However, for those who are *Shabbat* observers, these same laws serve to preserve the time and space of *Shabbat* as a special sacred time, untouched by day to day worries or concerns.

There is a freedom in our obligation to observe *Shabbat*. We don't think about work, there is no concern about tests; we are not intruded upon by commercialism. There is freedom to sit with friends, talk with family, be undisturbed by phone calls, or other outside intrusions. There is liberation in the rest and rejuvenation of *Shabbat*.

Think About This:

You are a high school student in a highly competitive public school, and you regularly observe *Shabbat*. You get lots of homework and are stressed about this—especially on *Shabbat* when you think about all the work you have to do. How does keeping *Shabbat* affect your freedom? What choices do you have? What choices don't you have? What can you do to make *Shabbat* a celebration of your freedom rather than an imposition in your life?

You are a member of USY attending a *Shabbaton* in the middle of the winter. You and your three friends have gathered in your host's home to light *Shabbat* candles before walking over for *Kabbalat Shabbat*. As the flames dance against the walls, you stare at the bright light and feel all your stress and worries of the past week melt away. You know that for the next twenty-four hours you will pray, sing and eat with your closest friends. How is this *Shabbat* a celebration of spiritual freedom?

Observance of *Shabbat* is a testimony that God is the creator of the world. It is as if we are reminded weekly that for six days a week we can struggle to attain control over the world, but on the seventh day we rest, and are reminded that this world is God's creation. By observing *Shabbat*, we are reminded of our dependence on God. That is why our *Shabbat* is meant to be a day on which we stress peace, harmony and spirituality.

שֵׁשֶׁת יָמִים תַּעֲבֹד וְעָשִׂיתָ כָּל־מְלַאכְתֶּךָ: יוֹם
הַשְּׁבִיעִי שַׁבָּת לַיהוָה אֱלֹהֶיךָ לֹא־תַעֲשֶׂה כָל־מְלָאכָה אַתָּה |
וּבִנְךָ וּבִתֶּךָ עַבְדְּךָ וַאֲמָתְךָ וּבְהֶמְתֶּךָ וְגֵרְךָ אֲשֶׁר בִּשְׁעָרֶיךָ:

"Six days you shall labor and do all your work, but the seventh day is
a Sabbath to Adonai your God, you shall not do any work."
(Exodus 20:9-10)

What effect does this have on personal freedom? Are there Shabbat mitzvot that liberate your life when you observe them?

_____

_____

_____

_____

_____

Until the introduction of a day of rest, humanity for the most part worked from dawn to dusk, day after day, week after week, with no rest. The renowned psychologist, Erich Fromm, hailed *Shabbat* as a one-day release from 'the chains of time'. Although Judaism has retained a unique set of rules and regulations surrounding the day of rest, the concept of a weekly day of rest has now become universal.

What are the tradeoffs between personal freedom and religious life?

דרור יקרא *21*

Dror Yikra

"Freedom for one and all is God's behest as *Shabbat* was created for repose and for rest; Seek my sanctuary, my sacred place, Give me a pledge of redemption and grace. Heed my people's cry, show me a sign, in vineyards of hope plant a fruitful vine. Repel all my foes; cause them to fall. Hear my voice, Eternal One, when I call. Make the wilderness flourish in fertility, To all who observe *Shabbat*, grant prosperity. Make wisdom your crown *mitzvot* at your side, Let *Shabbat* be your treasure, its joy your pride."
(*Siddur Sim Shalom*)

דְּרוֹר יִקְרָא לְבֵן וּלְבַת,
וְיִנְצָרְכֶם כְּמוֹ בָבַת,
נְעִים שִׁמְכֶם וְלֹא יֻשְׁבַּת,
שְׁבוּ נוּחוּ בְּיוֹם שַׁבָּת.

דְּרֹשׁ נָוִי וְאוּלַמִּי,
וְאוֹת יֶשַׁע עֲשֵׂה עִמִּי,
נְטַע שׂוֹרֵק בְּתוֹךְ כַּרְמִי,
שְׁעֵה שַׁוְעַת בְּנֵי עַמִּי.

דְּרֹךְ פּוּרָה בְּתוֹךְ בָּצְרָה,
וְגַם בָּבֶל אֲשֶׁר גָּבְרָה,
נְתֹץ צָרַי בְּאַף עֶבְרָה,
שְׁמַע קוֹלִי בְּיוֹם אֶקְרָא.

אֱלֹהִים תֵּן בְּמִדְבָּר הַר,
הֲדַס שִׁטָּה בְּרוֹשׁ תִּדְהָר,
וְלַמַּזְהִיר וְלַנִּזְהָר,
שְׁלוֹמִים תֵּן כְּמֵי נָהָר.

הֲדֹךְ קָמַי, אֵל קַנָּא,
בְּמוֹג לֵבָב וּבִמְגִנָּה,
וְנַרְחִיב פֶּה נְמַלֵּא נָא
לְשׁוֹנֵנוּ לְךָ רִנָּה.

דְּעֵה חָכְמָה לְנַפְשֶׁךָ,
וְהִיא כֶתֶר לְרֹאשֶׁךָ,
נְצֹר מִצְוַת קְדוֹשֶׁךָ,
שְׁמֹר שַׁבַּת קָדְשֶׁךָ.

Who do you think this *zemer* (song) was speaking to? What is the message?

_____
_____
_____

What in the text might serve such a purpose?

_____
_____
_____

The tension of observance of *Shabbat* is not a new one for Jews. The above poem, sung as part of *Shabbat zmirot*, illustrates the tensions of those who observe *Shabbat*. This song celebrates the sacredness in the liberty of the *Shabbat rest*. It uses this opportunity to beseech of God that those who do observe *Shabbat* find prosperity. It must have been a tremendous hardship, in an agricultural society, to cease all work in the fields on *Shabbat*, to have faith in God that the crops would survive without constant supervision.

Despite the fact that there are tensions in the observance of *Shabbat*, it is clear that in the mind of this poet, *Shabbat* is also an ultimate expression of freedom. It is through *Shabbat* that one and all achieve a taste of true freedom, through the expression of pure rest, rest of the body and the soul.

Describe a Shabbat experience you have had that was one of total freedom, one of true rest and sanctity:

_____
_____

Compare your thoughts on the freedom of *Shabbat* with the following vision expressed by Rabbi Abraham Joshua Heschel:

> "To set apart one day a week for freedom, a day on which we would not use the instruments which have been so easily turned into weapons of destruction, a day for being with ourselves, a day of detachment from the vulgar, of independence of external obligations, a day on which we stop worshipping the idols of technical civilization, a day on which we use no money … is there any institution that holds out a greater hope for man's progress than the Sabbath?… The Sabbath itself is a sanctuary which we build, a sanctuary in time."
>
> *(Heschel, The Sabbath)*

Shabbat: Freedom to focus on what matters in life, to worship God

Freedom from daily worries

Freedom of the spirit

_____

_____

_____

Pesach: A Time to be Free

The holiday of Passover is considered the ultimate celebration of freedom in Jewish time. It is the telling of the historical freeing of the Jewish people from slavery, and is also considered the celebration of our spiritual freedom.

Pesach, also known as *zman heiruteinu*, the season of our liberation, is a time when we are commanded to recreate the experience of leaving slavery, of liberation from bondage and becoming a free people

Pesach—God–Given Freedom

> *We were Pharaoh's slaves in Egypt, and the Lord our God brought us forth from there with a mighty hand and an outstretched arm. (Passover Haggadah)*

This is inarguably one of the prettiest images of God that we have in liturgical text. The strength and power of The Almighty, reaching out to take us out of Egypt conjures up thoughts of muscle and might. And yet, the idea of God reaching out and lifting each of us up from Egypt, placing us gently in a mighty hand and carrying us to freedom is also an awesomely gentle image of love and care. We experience a communal deliverance performed on a personal level. In this text, freedom is not something that we earn, and it is not something inherent in our being. Freedom is delivered to us, as a personal gift from God.

Being slaves in Egypt is something that has touched our lives as Jews, permanently. Our annual reenactment of this slavery reminds us of the humanity that we share with all people. Our redemption at the hand of God also has left a permanent mark. We were set free by God, and will never be slaves again. We are empowered to guarantee our own freedom, and are called to action against all restrictions of freedom.

Close your eyes and imagine yourself caught somewhere, unable to get out. Picture God's hand reaching out and freeing you.

What are you feeling as God liberates you?

What does God's hand feel like as it lifts you to freedom?

God's role in our redemption is so emphasized in the retelling of the *Pesach* narrative in the Haggadah, that the roles played by Moses, Miriam and Aaron are virtually absent there. *Pesach* is the first step towards the covenant between God and the people, a covenant established at Mt. Sinai, and culminating in Israel's entrance to the Land of Israel. God's 'right' to choose us in this covenant is established when God's hand stretches out to save us in Egypt.

How does the absence of Moses, Miriam and Aaron in the Haggadah affect its message?

_____

_____

_____

What would the difference have been if a human had been the vehicle to transmit the ideas of freedom to Israel?

_____

_____

_____

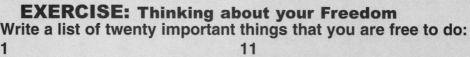

EXERCISE: Thinking about your Freedom
Write a list of twenty important things that you are free to do:

1	11
2	12
3	13
4	14
5	15
6	16
7	17
8	18
9	19
10	20

Now, go back and cross out anything you could not do it you were a slave.

How would you feel if you were prevented from doing these things?

Which things if taken away would cause you to:
        -protest peacefully?
        -protest, at the risk of jail?
        -protest at the risk of life?
        -leave your home with nothing but a suitcase and settle in another state or country?

בכל דור ודור חייב אדם לראות את עצמו כאלו הוא יצא ממצרים

> In each and every generation a person must see her/himself as if actually coming out of Egypt... It was not only our ancestors who the Holy One redeemed, but all of us as well were redeemed along with them.
>
> *(Passover Haggadah)*

DID YOU KNOW: Israel's redemption from Egypt is considered central to Jewish theology. It is mentioned in the first of the Ten Commandments, in the liturgy of the Friday night service, and in our daily liturgy including Shacharit, Maa'riv as well as the Kiddush.

The *Pesach* narrative teaches us that there are always possibilities for change in our lives. Until the Exodus it was a common belief that one born a slave would remain one throughout life. The Exodus from Egypt challenged the idea of permanent identity. Things do not have to remain as they are. We have the power to change the world that we inhabit, we have the ability to change our personal destinies. God has shown us in the story of *Pesach* that radical change is possible.

Do you know stories of individuals or communities that demonstrate the transformative power of change?

Individuals	Communities
1.	1.
2.	2.
3.	3.

We must each view ourselves as being redeemed, as being freed by God. Our freedom is reenacted annually. The empowering message of Passover is that freedom is an ongoing process. There will always be moments in our lives when we need to find freedom. There are many different types of slavery that we will encounter in our lives. It is through the vehicle of faith that we are able to find our redemption. If we allow God in our lives, then we allow ourselves the chance to experience coming out of Egypt, we allow God to deliver us from slavery to freedom.

How are you enslaved (compelled, subjugated) in your life today?

_____

_____

_____

What commitments do you have that you are not free to break, yet want to?

_____

_____

_____

How do you think God can help bring you to freedom?

_____

_____

_____

Other Reasons for the Pesach Freedom

דרש רב עוירא: בשכר נשים צדקניות שהיו באותו הדור -
נגאלו ישראל ממצרים

Israel was redeemed from Egypt on account of the righteous women of that generation.

(*Babylonian Talmud, Sotah 11b*)

The commentators explain that the righteous women of this generation remained loyal to their husbands and would aid and encourage them, and it was in this way that they preserved the existence of Israel.

אמר ר אלעזר הקפר בזכות ארבעה
דברים נגאלו ישראל ממצרים , שלא שינו את שמם, ולא שינו את
לשונם, ולא גילו את מסתורין שלהם, ולא היו פרוצים בעריות.

For four reasons were the children of Israel redeemed from Egypt: they did not change their names, they did not change their language, they did not reveal their secrets, and they were not promiscuous.

(*Midrash Tehilim 114:4*)

Compare the reasons provided in the two sources for Israel being freed from Egypt. Which one(s) seem most valid to you?

_____

_____

_____

The theme of redemption was a primary one in Rabbinic literature. The Talmudic Rabbis had different ideas about what led to the redemption. We can learn from the two sources that the understanding of the redemption was to view it as a reward for outstanding moral behavior. The righteous women defied the rules of the land and saved the Jewish infants who were being threatened with death. The Children of Israel did not buckle under their oppression and maintained their religious independence through language and ritual. Although it was on account of their behaviors, it is always God who is the vehicle to this freedom.

The centrality of God to our freedom is best expressed in the opening statement of the *Aseret Dibrot*– the Ten Commandments. This central document in the Torah proclaims that our belief in God is connected to the Exodus from Egypt.

אָנֹכִי יְהֹוָה אֱלֹהֶיךָ אֲשֶׁר הוֹצֵאתִיךָ מֵאֶרֶץ מִצְרַיִם מִבֵּית עֲבָדִים:

"I am the Lord your God who brought you out of the land of Egypt, the house of bondage."

(*Exodus 20:2*)

The Exodus from Egypt serves as a reminder of faith. God, who brought us out of Egypt, God who redeemed us from slavery, is God who we are commanded to believe in. Similarly, we, the Jewish people have reason to believe in God, because we experience life as if we ourselves were taken out of Egypt, as if we ourselves experienced the miracle of freedom by God's hand directly.

Matzah - A Symbol of Pesach Freedom

The greatest symbol of freedom on Passover is the matzah. Is matzah the bread of slaves or the bread of a free person? Is this the cheap but filling food that the slaves ate, or the bread of liberation? Is matzah a symbol of slavery or freedom? Matzah has a dual nature. It is transformed from a bread of the slave to the sustenance of the free. It journeys from slavery to freedom. It carries the pockmarked surface of one who has suffered the blows of the taskmaster, but it survives unbroken.

Before reading the texts below, can you recall the two different reasons for eating matzah on *Pesach*?

> And they baked unleavened cakes of the dough that they had taken out of Egypt, for it was not leavened, since they had been driven out of Egypt and could not delay, nor had they prepared any provisions for themselves. *(Exodus 12:39)*

> You shall not eat anything leavened with it, for seven days you shall eat unleavened bread, bread of distress, so that you may remember the day of your departure from the land of Egypt as long as your live. *(Deuteronomy 16:3)*

How can matzah symbolize both slavery and freedom?

_____

_____

_____

Which description would you choose for matzah, bread of affliction or bread of freedom? Can you think of another description?

_____

_____

_____

Pesach—Freedom to Action

The *Pesach* journey took the Israelites out of Egypt, through the desert, to Mt. Sinai. The journey took them from slavery to freedom. The experience of freedom is tied closely into the journey towards receiving the Torah.

Let's look at this text again:

והלוחות מעשה אלהים המה והמכתב מכתב אלהים הוא חרות על הלוחות.
אל תקרא חרות אלא חרות. שאין לך בן חורין אלא מי שעוסק בתלמוד תורה.

> Rabbi Yehoshua ben Levi taught: it is written: "And the tablets were the work of God, graven (*harut*) upon the tablets" Do not read *harut* (graven) but rather *herut* (freedom), for no person is free except one who engages in the study of Torah. *(Pirkei Avot 6:2)*

This is the bread of affliction, *lehem oni,* which our ancestors ate as slaves in the land of Egypt.
(Passover Haggadah)

List three things that are liberating about the study of Torah.

Think About This:

You are a member of a *bikkur holim* group in your local synagogue. It is the custom of your group to spend the week before *Pesach* visiting local hospitals and elderly residences delivering *Pesach* food and reading through portions of the *Pesach Haggadah*.

As you read the following situations, think about these questions:

—What freedoms do they have?

—What choices exist?

—Did these people come to their present situation because of a choice they were free to make?

You meet a teenage girl on the cancer floor of the hospice center. The girl only has a limited number of weeks left to live. She wants to know how she can thank God on Pesach for freeing her from slavery when for most of her life she has been a slave to cancer and is now dying of it.
Where is her freedom?

You meet a teenage boy who was struck by a drunk driver on his way home from school. Although he is alive, he has lost use of both legs, and will be in a wheelchair the rest of his life. He wants to know how he is going to thank God for taking him out of slavery to freedom, when he feels he has just lost his freedom.
What is his freedom?

You meet a young child who is in the hospital suffering from malnutrition. This child's family has been homeless since the start of the year. The child has never seen a pair of new jeans that hadn't been worn by others first, and hasn't had a square meal in months. How is this child's family going to respond to the idea that on *Pesach* God granted us all freedom?
Where is their freedom?

The Israelites needed God for their first taste of freedom. God gave us the Torah as a tool to help us continue to create and guarantee freedom in the world. One message of *Pesach* is to use our freedom to free others. We needed God for our first taste of liberation. Having experienced this freedom, we were transformed as a people. God has now left the task of bringing about redemption to our own powers. Today we ask all who are deprived to join us in recalling the obligation towards liberation, all who are hungry to join us in eating. **MAZON**, a Jewish response to hunger, has the following powerful message about *Pesach*.

A Call to Action— MAZON: A Jewish Response to Hunger

MAZON ("food" in Hebrew) raises funds principally from Jews nationwide who donate 3% of the cost of weddings, bar and bat mitzvahs and other joyous events. Other funds come from annual Passover and High Holy Days appeals and thousands of commemorative contributions. Three percent: to a cost of $1,000, add $30; to $5,000 add $150; to $10,000 add $300.

With these contributions **MAZON** provides cash grants to a broad spectrum of nonprofit organizations working to confront the tragedy of hunger, primarily in the U.S. but also in Israel and in impoverished countries. Our dual purpose is to provide for those who are hungry today as well as to help alleviate the poverty that causes hunger. Since our founding in 1985, **MAZON** has granted over $17 million to hundreds of programs.

MAZON funds a variety of organizations: food banks and food pantries in inner cities and rural areas; kosher meals-on-wheels programs for homebound elderly people; multi-service centers that provide poor, hungry and homeless families with food, shelter and counseling; state and national organizations that conduct research and education activities and work for the kind of public policies that can bring about long-term solutions to hunger.

How We Raise Funds

In addition to the 3% concept described above, **MAZON** asks American Jews to continue the ancient Jewish tradition of feeding the hungry by:

—sharing the joy of festive occasions by contributing 3% of the cost of life-cycle celebrations contributing

—at Yom Kippur — the most solemn day of the Jewish year — the money that would have been spent on food during the single day of voluntary fasting, to help feed those whose fast shows no sign of ending

—at Passover, letting "one who is hungry enter and eat" by giving to **MAZON** the amount of money that would have been spent to invite one extra person to the Seder table

—giving to **MAZON** to commemorate happy occasions in the lives of friends and family members, or to honor the memory of loved ones

How You Can Help

Our ancestors left the corners of their fields for the needy. You can follow in their footsteps by sending **MAZON** 3% of the cost of your celebrations throughout the year: birthdays, anniversaries, b'nai mitzvah parties, weddings, baby namings — any joyous occasion. For most of us, 3% is the corners of our fields. For a hungry person, it is the gift of life.

On Yom Kippur, you can respond to Isaiah's charge to "share your bread with the hungry" by providing to **MAZON** the dollars you ordinarily would spend to feed your family. Deepen the meaning of this voluntary fast by helping to alleviate endless days of involuntary fast — the fast of the poor.

During Passover, you can remember that we were strangers in the land of Egypt, and respond to the needs of the hungry stranger today by sending to **MAZON** the dollars that you would have spent to feed one extra guest at your seder. Add meaning to the words of the Haggadah: "Let all who are hungry enter and eat."

The rabbis taught, "Bread is the comfort of the heart." You can offer comfort to those who mourn with a contribution honoring the memory of loved ones. You can also honor friends or family with a contribution to celebrate their joyous occasions.

To contribute make your check payable to MAZON and send to:
MAZON: A Jewish Response to Hunger
12401 Wilshire Blvd., Suite 303
Los Angeles, CA 90025

Pesach:

Freedom to be *bnai horin* (free individuals)

Freedom from slavery

Freedom of our people, and of individuals

Yovel: A Time to be Free

"Take my hand
come with me
Where the children
are free
And I say it ain't far
To this land from
where we are
Take my hand come
along
Lend your voice to
my song
Come along take my
hand and we'll sing
In a land where the
children are free..."

A shofar is blown in town. People begin streaming out of their homes, thanking God for loaning this land to them for the last 50 years. In appreciation of this loan, a slave is freed in one house on the corner. Another household across the street returns a field that it had acquired when the bank foreclosed on property owned by a poor family. The field will now return to this poor couple, and with its fruits they will begin to restore their lives and sustain themselves.

For the next year, the community will not trade in their agricultural goods, allowing the land some time off to rest. There will be acts of loving kindness and a community that together will have to share in order to survive. This will be a place that knows that one good gesture breeds another. This will be a community that knows that if even one individual is not free, then God is not free.

This is a free-hand depiction of the concept of *Yovel,* the Jubilee, the fiftieth year when the land of Israel is restored to its previous ownership, a restoration that occurs between humans and humans with land, finances and freedom, and between the Jewish people and God. Slaves go free, debts are rescinded, and family homesteads are returned to their original owners. Because it is also the Sabbatical year (the *shmita*), the land rests from physical labor as well.

וְקִדַּשְׁתֶּם אֵת שְׁנַת הַחֲמִשִּׁים שָׁנָה וּקְרָאתֶם

דְּרוֹר בָּאָרֶץ לְכָל־יֹשְׁבֶיהָ יוֹבֵל הִוא תִּהְיֶה לָכֶם וְשַׁבְתֶּם אִישׁ

אֶל־אֲחֻזָּתוֹ וְאִישׁ אֶל־מִשְׁפַּחְתּוֹ תָּשֻׁבוּ׃ יוֹבֵל הִוא שְׁנַת

הַחֲמִשִּׁים שָׁנָה תִּהְיֶה לָכֶם לֹא תִזְרָעוּ וְלֹא תִקְצְרוּ

אֶת־סְפִיחֶיהָ וְלֹא תִבְצְרוּ אֶת־נְזִרֶיהָ׃ יבִּי יוֹבֵל הִוא קֹדֶשׁ

תִּהְיֶה לָכֶם מִן־הַשָּׂדֶה תֹּאכְלוּ אֶת־תְּבוּאָתָהּ׃

"And you shall hallow the fiftieth year. You shall proclaim release throughout the land for all its inhabitants. It shall be a jubilee for you: each of you shall return to his holdings and each of you shall return to his family. That fiftieth year shall be jubilee for you: you shall not sow, neither shall you reap the aftergrow or harvest the untrimmed vines for it is is jubilee. It shall be holy to you..."
(Leviticus 25:10-12)

What would happen if we forgive all debts and return land to previous owners every fifty years?

All too often this text is treated as a Biblical fantasy. Would you be willing to give up your property and restore it to its original owner? How many banks would forgive debt? How many communities would not work the fields for a year? How many of us would give up the status and power that we might have acquired in order to restore social equality? These are all ideas that the *Yovel*, the Jubilee, asks us to consider. This is what we are asked to do by God.

EXERCISE: What might be components of a modern Yovel (Jubilee)? Compare the examples from the Torah's description of the Yovel with what you think would happen today:

TORAH	TODAY
release for all inhabitants	_____
return to your families	_____
return to your holdings	_____
do not sow	_____
do not reap the growth or the untrimmed vines	_____
when selling land, charge only for years remaining until yovel	_____

In today's terms, "Proclaim Liberty" could mean freeing oneself from the bondage of acquisition; the race to own the most property, the best clothing, the prettiest car, the largest house. When what you have acquired from others or at their expense is restored to them as a foundation of your community, then that is a place of freedom.

וקראתם דרור בארץ, בארץ אין,
בחוצה לארץ לא, תלמוד לומר: יובל היא, מכל
מקום. אם כן, מה תלמוד לומר בארץ? בזמן שהדרור נוהג בארץ -
נוהג בחוצה לארץ, אין דרור נוהג בארץ - אינו נוהג בחוצה לארץ.

"And you shall proclaim liberty in the land - in the land - meaning in the land of Israel jubilee shall happen, but in any other land it shall not happen." (Babylonian Talmud, Kiddushin 38b)

This text acts in a classic Talmudic manner of limitation. The Rabbinic assumption is that text is never redundant. Every word is meant to teach something. In this particular instance the Hebrew letter "*bet*" is a teacher. By indicating specifically that "*ba'aretz*" (meaning "*in* Israel") we must observe the *Yovel*, the Rabbis are able to understand the text in a limiting fashion. *Only in this land, the land of Israel, are we under this obligation, not in any other land.* Furthermore, it can only happen in this land when Jews are the owners of the land. This limitation also creates an idyllic notion of the *Yovel*. After all, how often do all Jews dwell in and own the land of Israel?

This text reflects the difficult time some Rabbis from Talmudic times had with the concept of *Yovel*. Rather than dismiss the notion, they limited it. They no longer viewed the *Yovel* as an actual occurrence that the Jewish community would experience every fifty years. Instead the *Yovel* became part of an ideal that would only be experienced when the Jewish people returned to ownership of the Land of Israel. In other words, *Yovel* would be truly experienced in the age of the Messiah.

Dar—to dwell, to live;

medayer—one who lives there, one who dwells;

sounds like dror—freedom

Embedded in the dialogue limiting the implication of the Jubilee year is a minority voice with a different opinion about yovel.

Let's take another look at this text:

דתניא: אין דרור אלא לשון חירות. אמר רבי
יהודה מה לשון דרור - כמדייר בי דיירא, ומוביל סחורה בכל מדינה.

> "*Dror* (liberty) is none other than the language of freedom. Rabbi Yehudah says - what is this language of *dror*? To teach us that *dror* is when a person can live where that person chooses (be *medayer*, from the root phonetic *dror*) and be able to trade in any country." (*Babylonian Talmud, Rosh HaShana 9b*)

How does Rabbi Yehudah transform the notion of yovel into one that could be applicable in any society?

_____

_____

_____

"Proclaim liberty throughout the land" is interpreted to mean a situation whereby any person can live with freedom where he or she chooses, and each individual has the potential to conduct business wherever he or she may want. By transposing the root '*dor*', from '*dror*' as freedom to '*dar*' as dwelling, Rabbi Yehudah is able to transform and expand the implication of the Jubilee year. Rabbi Yehuda is saying: even though we cannot practice all the rules that are related to the *Yovel* by virtue of not being in the Land of Israel, still there is value to the moral message of the *Yovel*, to the concept of freedom, and we must learn from that.

What are other messages that you learn from yovel that you might be able to translate to any society?

_____

_____

_____

Yovel:
Freedom to create economic and social liberty

Freedom from the burden of monetary possessions

Freedom of time, freedom of the land, freedom of people

Yovel is about creating a sanctified world by acknowledging that what we own was never really ours in the first place. It is about declaring freedom for all individuals; not just for those who have earned it, or have paid for it, not for specific classes, or communities. The *Yovel* provides freedom by reminding us that all these possessions are not really ours to 'own'. They are God's. And God has made a simple request: God has asked us to create sacred time and space through the sacred action of returning social and economic justice to the world.

Through the *Yovel*, we sanctify eternal time, God's ownership of the world we live in. Perhaps we can also see *Yovel* sanctifying mundane time: learning to carve out one hour a week when we volunteer to tutor an inner-city child, when we work in a soup kitchen, when we extend ourselves in some way. By doing these deeds, we are expressing our freedom to act in God's image.

EXERCISE: List some ways you can create freedom for yourself or for others:

HOME

_____

_____

_____

_____

SCHOOL

_____

_____

_____

_____

TOWN

_____

_____

_____

COUNTRY

_____

_____

_____

A Call to Action— A Call for an International Jubilee 2000
Resolution in Support of International Debt Relief

WHEREAS the world's poorest nations bear a crushing debt of more than $2 trillion borrowed from the world's richest nations, from multilateral organizations and from private banks in the richest countries; and

WHEREAS these poor nations' debt service payments often dwarf their spending on programs that would improve their citizens' lives, such as Bolivia which in 1998 spent 17 times more on debt service than on rural clean water and sanitation programs, or Nicaragua, which in 1997 sent more than 50 percent of all government revenue to wealthier nations and banks for debt service, or Mozambique, which now spends four times more on debt service than on health services, even though 25 percent of its children die before age five; and

WHEREAS all African nations combined paid 31 percent more in debt service than they received from wealthier countries as aid, and paid the International Monetary Fund $600 million more in debt service than they received as loans; and

WHEREAS these debts encourage poor nations to exploit their natural resources, tolerate exploitive labor practices and promote emigration and social instability; and

WHEREAS U.S. President Clinton, the World Bank, the New York Times, among many other leading political and civic organizations agree that debt relief is needed to lift the poor nations from poverty, and support this effort; and

WHEREAS world religious leaders have joined in support of this effort; and

WHEREAS we find in the Torah the institution of the *Yovel*, or jubilee, whereby citizens are afforded the opportunity of a fresh economic start every 50 years; and

WHEREAS Maimonides rules that the noblest tzedakah is that which enables the poor to attain economic independence.

THEREFORE BE IT RESOLVED that the Rabbinical Assembly supports the international effort to call on wealthy nations to forgive the impossible debt of poor nations.

BE IT FURTHER RESOLVED that the Rabbinical Assembly calls upon the leaders of the nations that will benefit from debt relief to assure that the funds formerly designated for debt servicing be used for direct welfare and relief.

Recommended by the Rabbinical Assembly Plenum to the Executive Council and passed June 2000

The Rabbinical Assembly
The international association of Conservative rabbis; Determines the Conservative interpretation of Jewish law through its **Committee on Jewish Law and Standards**; coordinates rabbinic efforts on behalf of Israel and social action projects; and runs a number of other activities for the educational, social and professional welfare of its members.

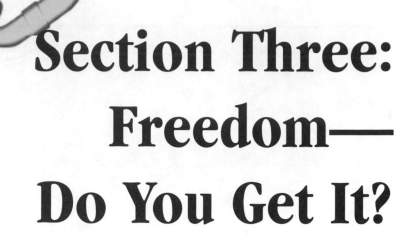

Section Three: Freedom— Do You Get It?

We do not wake up one morning and find a beautifully wrapped package waiting at our feet to be unwrapped, and within it the gift of freedom. How do we get our freedom? In some cases the answer is that we are born with the right to freedom. For others freedom is something to be fought for and won. Still others view freedom as a responsibility given by a governing body and regulated so that the community not suffer. This section will examine different sources of freedom. It will delve into the question of whether chosenness or obligation to *mitzvot* is an imposition on our freedom as individuals, or the ultimate expression of our freedom through our relationship with God.

Where does freedom come from?

Freedom is not an abstract philosophical idea. Freedom is a state of being. In Jewish history and in general world history we encounter battles for freedom. In political and social writings we are introduced to different realities of freedom. Where does this endowment of freedom derive from? Are we given our freedoms? Can they be taken away from us? In this section we will explore the sources of our freedoms, and some of the conflicts that arise when we try to understand how we achieve/ acquire or accept our freedoms.

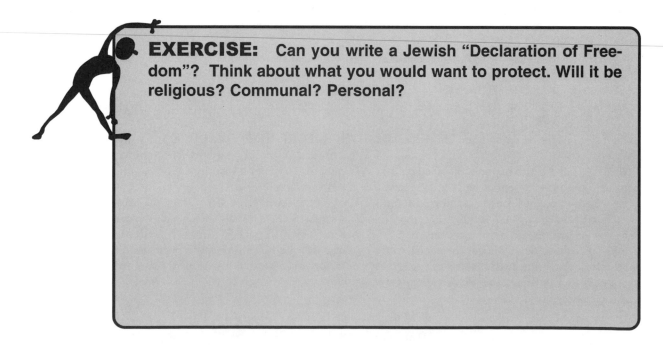

EXERCISE: Can you write a Jewish "Declaration of Freedom"? Think about what you would want to protect. Will it be religious? Communal? Personal?

United States Declaration of Independence

IN CONGRESS, July 4, 1776.
The unanimous Declaration of the thirteen United States of America,

When in the course of human events, it becomes necessary for one people to dissolve the political bands which have connected them with another, and to assume among the powers of the earth, the separate and equal station to which the Laws of Nature and of Nature's God entitle them, a decent respect to the opinions of mankind requires that they should declare the causes which impel them to the separation.

We hold these truths to be self-evident, that all men are created equal, that they are endowed by their Creator with certain unalienable Rights, that among these are Life, Liberty and the pursuit of Happiness.

—That to secure these rights, Governments are instituted among Men, deriving their just powers from the consent of the governed,

—That whenever any Form of Government becomes destructive of these ends, it is the Right of the People to alter or to abolish it, and to institute new Government, laying its foundation on such principles and organizing its powers in such form, as to them shall seem most likely to effect their Safety and Happiness. Prudence, indeed, will dictate that Governments long established should not be changed for light and transient causes; and accordingly all experience hath shewn, that mankind are more disposed to suffer, while evils are sufferable, than to right themselves by abolishing the forms to which they are accustomed…

Canadian Charter of Rights and Freedoms

Whereas Canada is founded upon principles that recognize the supremacy of God and the rule of law:

Guarantee of Rights and Freedoms

1. The Canadian Charter of Rights and Freedoms guarantees the rights and freedoms set out in it subject only to such reasonable limits prescribed by law as can be demonstrably justified in a free and democratic society.

Fundamental freedoms

2. Everyone has the following fundamental freedoms:
a) freedom of conscience and religion;
b) freedom of thought, belief, opinion and expression, including freedom of the press and other media of communication;
c) freedom of peaceful assembly; and
d) freedom of association.

Democratic rights of citizens

3. Every citizen of Canada has the right to vote in an election of members of the House of Commons or of a legislative assembly and to be qualified for membership therein.

Life, liberty and security of person

7. Everyone has the right to life, liberty and security of the person and the right not to be deprived thereof except in accordance with the principles of fundamental justice.

15. (1) Every individual is equal before and under the law and has the right to the equal protection and equal benefit of the law without discrimination and, in particular, without discrimination based on race, national or ethnic origin, colour, religion, sex, age or mental or physical disability.

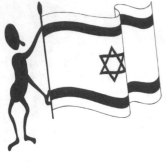

Megillat Ha'Atzmaut of the State of Israel:

Accordingly we, members of the People's Council, representatives of the Jewish Community of Eretz-Israel and of the Zionist Movement, are here assembled on the day of the termination of the British Mandate over Eretz-Israel and, by virtue of our natural and historic right and on the strength of the resolution of the United Nations General Assembly, hereby declare the establishment of a Jewish state in Eretz-Israel, to be known as the State of Israel.

We declare that, with effect from the moment of the termination of the Mandate being tonight, the eve of Sabbath, the 6th Iyar, 5708 (15th May, 1948), until the establishment of the elected, regular authorities of the State in accordance with the Constitution which shall be adopted by the Elected Constituent Assembly not later than the 1st October 1948, the People's Council shall act as a Provisional Council of State, and its executive organ, the People's Administration, shall be the Provisional Government of the Jewish State, to be called "Israel."

The State of Israel will be open for Jewish immigration and for the Ingathering of the Exiles; it will foster the development of the country for the benefit of all its inhabitants; it will be based on freedom, justice and peace as envisaged by the prophets of Israel; it will ensure complete equality of social and political rights to all its inhabitants irrespective of religion, race or sex; it will guarantee freedom of religion, conscience, language, education and culture; it will safeguard the Holy Places of all religions; and it will be faithful to the principles of the Charter of the United Nations.

Compare the Declaration of Independence of the United States of America, and the Charter Bill of Rights of Canada with the Megillat Ha'Atzmaut of the State of Israel.

EXERCISE
Who are the people in each declaration declaring freedom?

United States: _____
Canada: _____
Israel: _____

What are the sources of authority that the writers identify with allowing themselves to make each declaration?

	CANADA	UNITED STATES	ISRAEL
1			
2			
3			

What freedoms does each declaration say it will guarantee?

	CANADA	UNITED STATES	ISRAEL
1			
2			
3			

GOD–GIVEN FREEDOM

Freedom might be a part of our genetic make up. Freedom might be something that was included in our creation. Did God create us with the freedom to choose between good and evil? Do we have an innate freedom of distinction within us?

In the beginning, when Adam and Eve were in the Garden of Eden, they were given strict instructions by God:

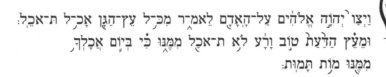

וַיְצַו יְהוָה אֱלֹהִים עַל־הָאָדָם לֵאמֹר מִכֹּל עֵץ־הַגָּן אָכֹל תֹּאכֵל׃
וּמֵעֵץ הַדַּעַת טוֹב וָרָע לֹא תֹאכַל מִמֶּנּוּ כִּי בְּיוֹם אֲכָלְךָ
מִמֶּנּוּ מוֹת תָּמוּת׃

> "And the Lord, God, commanded the human, saying, of every tree of the garden you are free to eat, but as for the tree of knowledge of good and bad, you must not eat of it, for as soon as you eat of it you shall die." (Genesis 2:16-17)

What do we learn about freedom when God issues an order to humans of how to behave?

_____
_____
_____

What do we learn from the behavior of Adam and Eve about God's ability to enforce this warning?

_____
_____
_____

What do we learn about the freedom of choice if Adam and Eve were able to eat from the tree?

_____
_____
_____

Some commentators claim that Adam and Eve's banishment from the Garden of Eden was caused by the humans' disobeyment of God's commandment. Alongside the banishment, humans acquired the ability to process choices. Other commentators maintain that humans were born with the ability to make choices, and that we were banished from the Garden because of a bad choice.

Humanity is born with the ability to experience freedom according to this story in Genesis. This is demonstrated first by God's need to indicate which trees can and cannot be touched, and what the consequences would be. If humans had not been created with freedom, there would be no need for God to warn of consequences of misbehaving because the humans would be incapable of defying God's will.

Imagine the creation narrative if there was to be no freedom for humanity. What would the story be like? What might our lives be like? What would your experience of the world be if freedom was not inherent?

_____

_____

_____

מָה־אֱנוֹשׁ כִּי־תִזְכְּרֶנּוּ וּבֶן־אָדָם כִּי תִפְקְדֶנּוּ׃
וַתְּחַסְּרֵהוּ מְּעַט מֵאֱלֹהִים וְכָבוֹד וְהָדָר תְּעַטְּרֵהוּ׃ תַּמְשִׁילֵהוּ
בְּמַעֲשֵׂי יָדֶיךָ כֹּל שַׁתָּה תַחַת־רַגְלָיו

What is human that You have been mindful of him
mortal man that You have taken note of him
that You have made him little less than divine
and adorned him with glory and majesty
You have made him master over your handiwork
laying the world at his feet.

(Psalms 8:5-7)

What responsibility do we have, according to this psalm?

_____

_____

_____

How does this responsibility affect our sense of freedom?

_____

_____

_____

Freedom according to this Psalm does not mean anarchy. The psalmist is very clear that in creating humanity in God's image, God bestowed upon humans the responsibility to care for the world that God created. There is an implication that this is a moral compulsion, not a limitation on one's freedom.

What would have happened if humanity was not created 'less divine' but 'equally divine' as God?

_____

_____

_____

What would have happened if humanity had the responsibility of the world 'thrust into our hands', rather than 'laid at our feet'?

_____

_____

_____

YETZER HATOV and YETZER HARA
INCLINATIONS AND IMPULSES

The language of *yetzer hatov/ hara* comes from the Biblical idea of human nature having an impulse to do good or evil. In the Talmud we find this idea developed as the Rabbis struggled with the tension between the two inclinations. Today we still find people who justify or explain inappropriate behaviors away by saying that their "bad side took over."

וַיֹּאמֶר יְהֹוָה אֶל־לִבּוֹ לֹא אֹסִף לְקַלֵּל עוֹד אֶת־הָאֲדָמָה בַּעֲבוּר הָאָדָם
כִּי יֵצֶר לֵב הָאָדָם רַע מִנְּעֻרָיו

> ...and the Lord reflected, musing: Never again will I doom the earth because of humanity, since the divisings of human's mind are evil from youth...
>
> *(Genesis 8:21)*

Following the flood, in the narrative of Noah, God regrets punishing the <u>land</u> for the behavior of humanity. The reflections of God in this narrative reflect the tension of Creation. God created a being that obviously was not fulfilling God's desires in the world. In the narrative about the flood God is on the angry verge of destroying this creation. Something holds God back, however, and this is a crucial moment. God realizes that having created humans with freedom, God cannot now punish them for not being perfect. The difficulty in this passage is the implication that humanity was created not with two inclinations, but with only an evil inclination.

God created humans with two inclinations

In response to this Biblical tradition, the Rabbis of the Talmudic age contended with the implication of humanity being created with an evil inclination. In Rabbinic thought we often find the view that humanity is created with two inclinations that the individual struggles with throughout life.

דרש רב נחמן בר רב חסדא: מאי דכתיב (בראשית ב)
וַיִּיצֶר ה אלהים את האדם בשני יודי ן -
שני יצרים ברא הקדוש ברוך הוא, אחד יֵצֶר טוֹב ואחר יֵצֶר רַע.

> Rabbi Nahman bar Rav Hisda explained in simple terms: When it is written "and God created (yiytzer) humanity" with two yods, it is because God created two inclinations, one a good inclination and one an evil inclination. (Babylonian Talmud, Berachot 61a)

In classic Talmudic style, Rabbi Nahman pays close attention to the smallest details of the Biblical text, learning from the existence of an additional letter in the word 'create', a lesson about the creation of humanity. According to this source, the two inclinations were a part of humanity from the start of Creation. God created us with the freedom to follow either inclination. Or, perhaps God limited our freedom by forcing us to contend with both inclinations.

Yetzer HaTov
"Good" inclinations; desire not to commit bad deeds

Yetzer HaRa
"Evil" inclinations; desire to commit bad needs

There is a complicated relationship between the Biblical text and Rabbinic thought. On the one hand all consider the Biblical text sacred. That said, the evolution of Rabbinic thought (referring here to the generations of Rabbis from the Talmudic period of the Babylonian Talmud, around the years 250-600 c.e.) brings with it a dynamic relationship with the Bible.

The Biblical text is authoritative, but Rabbinic theology remains independent. They utilize the text to explain, justify, limit and change the law, through precise reading of the text, with special attention paid to extra letters, redundant words, repetitive words, missing letters or words, and other nuances in the text.

The Rabbis are loyal to the Biblical text, but are comfortable adapting or changing the spirit of the law. Thus the theology reflected in the Biblical texts can be very different from the ideas put forth in the Rabbinic text.

Do you agree with this source that you were created with both inclinations, an evil one and a good one? Explain.

_____

_____

_____

Why did God created humans with two inclinations?

"Neither the angels nor the animals satisfied God; the former had no evil inclination, the latter had no good inclination. The good of the one and the evil of the other, therefore, are not the result of their free will. God therefore created humans who possesess both the good and the evil inclinations; if human follows evil, human is likened to an animal, if human follows good, human is higher than an angel."

Tanhuma

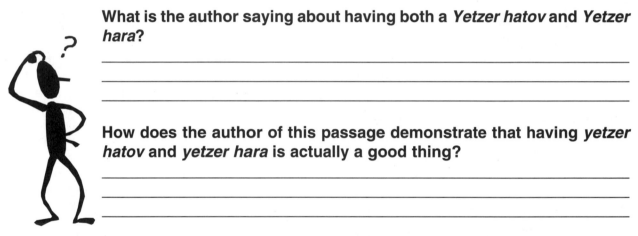

What is the author saying about having both a *Yetzer hatov* and *Yetzer hara*?

_____

_____

_____

How does the author of this passage demonstrate that having *yetzer hatov* and *yetzer hara* is actually a good thing?

_____

_____

_____

According to this narrative, the act of creation by God was to provide a creature that was a blend of good and evil. This narrative suggests that this blending provides each of us with the opportunity to be who we want and do as we want in this world. In this source the existence of an evil inclination is a gift that allows us to fulfill God's nccd to have a satisfying creature.

Nature of *yetzer hara*

ואיתימא רבי יהושע בן לוי: שבעה שמות יש לו ליצר הרע. הקדוש
ברוך הוא קראו רע, שנאמר (בראשית ח) כי יצר לב האדם רע
מנעוריו. משה קראו ערל, שנאמר (דברים י) ומלתם את ערלת
לבבכם. דוד קראו טמא שנאמר (תהלים נא) לב טהור ברא לי
אלהים - מכלל דאיכא טמא.

Yehoshua ben Levi said: Seven names has the *yetzer hara*: God called it "evil" רע, as it says: 'the nature of humanity is evil from youth' Moses called it "thickening," ערל as it says: 'cut away the thickening of your hearts' (Deut. 10:16)
David called it "impure," טמא as it says: 'fashion a pure heart for me God' (Psalms 51:12). From the general rule that a pure heart, implies that there are hearts that are impure.

For further study:

Take out a Hebrew Bible (Tanakh) and look at each of the stories that are mentioned in this source.

Compare and contrast the behavior of the people in each story.

How does this shed light on your understanding of *yetzer hara*?

שלמה קראו שונא, שנאמר (משלי כה)
אם רעב שנאך האכילהו לחם ואם צמא השקהו מים כי גחלים אתה
חותה על ראשו וה ישלם לך, אל תקרי ישלם לך אלא ישלימנו לך.
ישעיה קראו מכשול, שנאמר (ישעיהו נז) סולו סולו פנו דרך הרימו
מכשול מדרך עמי. יחזקאל קראו אבן, שנאמר (יחזקאל לו) והסרתי
את לב האבן מבשרכם ונתתי לכם לב בשר. יואל קראו צפוני,
שנאמר (יואל ב) ואת הצפוני ארחיק מעליכם.

Solomon called it "enemy," שונא as it says: 'if your enemy is hungry give him bread to eat.' (Proverbs 25:21)

Isaiah called it "an obstacle," מכשול as it says: 'clear a road, remove all obstacles' (Isaiah 57:14)

Ezekiel called it "a stone," אבן as it says: 'I will remove the heart of stone from your body' (Ezekiel 26:26)

Joel called it "northern," צפוני as it says: 'I will drive the northerner far from you' (Joel 2:20). For the North is the seat of evil in the body.

(Babylonian Talmud, Sukkah 52b)

What do we learn about the evil inclination from this text? What are its causes?

_____

_____

_____

Define the *yetzer hara* according to this source:

_____

_____

_____

What does the definition of *Yetzer Hara* from the Babylonian Talmud tell you about the *Yetzer HaTov*?

_____

_____

_____

EXERCISE: Create the qualities of yetzer hatov by writing the antonyms for the qualities given in the source from above:

Yetzer Hara	Yetzer Hatov
evil	_____
thickened	_____
impure	_____
enemy	_____
obstacle	_____
stone	_____
northern	_____

The evil inclination is a yoke that can hold humanity back from doing good. It is cold, it is heavy, it is hard, and it is not a desired part of our make up. The words used to describe the evil inclination are all taken from sources in which the Children of Israel have gone astray. In each source they have wronged God by turning away from the life of Torah. *Yetzer hara* in each of these cases represent the Children of Israel making a bad choice, using their freedom to do the wrong thing.

Rabbi Ashi says that *yetzer hara* seems like a delicate thread, but it becomes gradually stronger until it is as strong as rope.... As it says: there is a member in the human body (*yetzer hara*) which the more you satisfy the more hungry it becomes. But if you do not do its will and do not satisfy it, then it will become tired of your person and cease to lead you astray. *(Sefer HaMaaseh 150)*

Can you think of some (real-life) examples that support this text?

_____
_____
_____

Can you think of other bad habits that also seem to become more hungry the more you satisfy them? Does this allegory seem realistic to you?

_____
_____
_____

If *yetzer hara* is something the grows stronger in our midst, what freedom do we have to avoid it?

_____
_____
_____

כך הקב ה אמר להם לישראל: בני,
בראתי יצר הרע ובראתי לו תורה תבלין, ואם אתם עוסקים בתורה -
אין אתם נמסרים בידו

The Holy One of Blessed Being said to Israel: My children, I created yetzer hara, and I created for it the Torah as a solvent. And if you occupy yourselves with the study of Torah, then you will not be delivered to the evil inclination.

(Babylonian Talmud, Kiddushin 30b)

How can Torah study help you resist the *yetzer hara*?

_____
_____
_____

How is this a reflection of our freedom to make choices in our lives?

_____

_____

_____

This source makes explicit our earlier assumption that living a life of Torah will keep us from *yetzer hara*. God gives us the Torah as an antidote to the poison of *yetzer hara*. We do not have the freedom to entirely eliminate this inclination, but we have the freedom to determine the degree to which it will impact on our lives. We have and can choose to use the tools to control it. God has given us the freedom to make mistakes, and the freedom to do the right thing, the freedom to repent, the freedom to change, as well as guidelines so that we understand how to take the right path.

CHOSENNESS

God created humanity with the freedom to live whatever life they choose. God also bestowed on humans two inclinations, an evil one and a good one. Finally, God provided the Jewish people with a guideline so that they would know how to avoid the obstacles of the evil inclination. This special relationship is reflected in the concept of chosenness.

WHAT IS CHOSENNESS?

כִּי עַם קָדוֹשׁ אַתָּה לַיהוָה אֱלֹהֶיךָ בְּךָ בָּחַר |
יְהוָה אֱלֹהֶיךָ לִהְיוֹת לוֹ לְעַם סְגֻלָּה מִכֹּל הָעַמִּים אֲשֶׁר עַל־פְּנֵי הָאֲדָמָה׃

> For you are a people consecrated to the Lord your God; of all the peoples on earth, the Lord, your God chose you to be God's treasured people.

> *(Deuteronomy 7:6)*

If God has selected the Jews to be the 'chosen people' do we have any freedom to say no?

_____

_____

_____

What do you think about keeping a commitment you didn't make?

_____

_____

_____

The idea that God has made a special choice is a reflection of the idea of the covenant, the *brit*, between the people and God. There are many ways we might define this *brit*, and in all of the definitions the actual relationship between people and God is essential. The special relationship might contain unique privileges. There might be an imposition of extra obligations and responsibility. The motivation might be God's need for a vehicle in the world, or it could be altruistic, pure love. It carries promise of favorable consideration, the idea of rejection being unimaginable.

Is chosenness something you can "opt" for, or is it something imposed upon you?

EXERCISE: When I think of myself as a part of "The Chosen People" I think that....

Mark the appropriate place for each item below:

	Strongly Disagree				Strongly Agree	
I am special	1	2	3	4	5	6
I have a closer relationship with God	1	2	3	4	5	6
I am part of a closed club.	1	2	3	4	5	6
I have a different relationship with God than others do	1	2	3	4	5	6
I have greater responsibilities in the world than others do.	1	2	3	4	5	6
I have a better relationship with God than others do.	1	2	3	4	5	6
I am better than other people.	1	2	3	4	5	6
I will have a better life than other people.	1	2	3	4	5	6
God will protect me.	1	2	3	4	5	6
I will suffer more than other people	1	2	3	4	5	6
God loves me more	1	2	3	4	5	6
Being chosen is a burden	1	2	3	4	5	6

וַיִּקַּח סֵפֶר הַבְּרִית וַיִּקְרָא בְּאָזְנֵי הָעָם וַיֹּאמְרוּ כֹּל אֲשֶׁר־דִּבֶּר יְהֹוָה נַעֲשֶׂה וְנִשְׁמָע:

Then he took the record of the covenant and read it aloud to the people. And they said, all that the Lord has spoken we will do and we will listen.

(Exodus 24:7)

The Hebrew text says, na'aseh v'nishma, which literally means, we will do and we will listen. It's like signing a contract without reading it. What does it mean to do something and only listen after the action is done? Under what circumstances might you agree to something without knowing exactly what it is? What does that say about the relationship between you and the other person/ party?

_____

_____

_____

_____

God chose the Jews and we affirmed this choice when accepting God's Torah. We were endowed as humans with a sense of morality, and we were endowed as Jews with creative expression of peoplehood, passed to us through the living Torah. Our freedom is expressed in our choice to do God's will. The idea that the Jews accepted upon themselves the Torah, and through it this special relationship, is further developed in some Talmudic statements.

What does this say about the unique chosenness of the Jews?

> The nations of the world were asked to accept the Torah, in order that they should have no excuse for saying, had we been asked we would have accepted… God appeared to children of Esau the wicked and said to them, "Will you accept the Torah?" They said to God, "What is written in it?" God said to them, "You will not murder." Then they said in return, "The very heritage which our father left us was, and by thy sword live."
>
> God then appeared to the children of Amnon and Moab. God said to them, "Will you accept the Torah?" They said to God, "What is written in it?" God said, "You will not commit adultery." They however said to God that they were all children of adulterers, as they were the children of the daughters of Lot with their father.
>
> God then appeared to the children of Ishmael. God said to them, "Will you accept the Torah?" They said to God, "What is written in it?" God said, "You will not steal." They said to God, "The very blessing that was upon our father was to have his hand upon everything."
>
> God then came to the children of Israel and said, "Will you accept the Torah?" and they responded, "All that God has said we will do and obey."
>
> *(Mechilta de-Rabbi Yishmael, Masecheta Hachodesh, 5)*

The idea that the Jews accepted the Torah and the *brit* freely is emphasized by demonstrating the number of nations could have accepted it, but rejected the offer of this chosen relationship. There are no negative consequences when each nation rejects God's offer of the Torah. Israel is exalted in this text as the only nation willing to stand up and accept upon itself the yoke of Torah.

ואמר רב דימי בר חמא:
מלמד שכפה הקב ה הר כגיגית על ישראל, ואמר להם:
אם אתם מקבלין את התורה - מוטב, ואם לאו - שם תהא קבורתכם!

> Rav Dimi bar Hama said: This teaches us that God suspended the mountain over them like a vault, and said, 'if you accept the Torah it will be good, but if not here you will find your graves.'
>
> *(Babylonian Talmud, Avodah Zara 2b)*

Compare this text to the source from the *Mechilta*. What does each say about our freedom to choose to accept upon ourselves the Torah and *brit* with God?

The previous texts reflect the limitation on the freedom of the Children of Israel to be chosen by God. It suggests that God suspended the mountain over their heads, coercing them to 'choose' the Torah. The engagement in intimidation tactics is a very human characteristic bestowed upon God in this passage. It leaves open to the imagination the possibility that the Children of Israel might have chosen death over Torah, as doubtful as it is to us as an audience. Still the message is clear; God cannot absolutely force humans to do anything, there is still a freedom on the part of humanity, forcing God to engage in scare tactics. The Children of Israel exercised their freedom in becoming a part of God's *brit*, and in accepting the Torah as a way of life.

Think About This:

Imagine that you are standing at Mount Sinai. Are you prepared to accept upon yourself the unique status of being chosen by God to receive the Torah? What are you feeling at this moment?

_____

_____

_____

_____

_____

_____

_____

WHAT LIMITS OUR FREEDOM?

While the previous sources all indicate that humanity is given freedom from God, there is also a hint of the fact that this freedom is not always considered limitless. What are the limits on this freedom, and how far do these limits extend?

Free Will or God's Will?

A tension exists between our creation as beings with freedom, with two inclinations, with the ability to make intelligent choices, and with the belief in the existence of an absolute God who knows all and is all powerful. This tension is reflected in select Biblical and Talmudic text. However the primary writers about this subject are the philosophers of the Middle Ages, who bring us a rich and complicated understanding of the struggle with free will and God's will based upon the Biblical texts.

יָדַעְתִּי יְהוָֹה כִּי לֹא לָאָדָם דַּרְכּוֹ לֹא־לְאִישׁ הֹלֵךְ וְהָכִין אֶת־צַעֲדוֹ׃

If humans do not direct their own steps, who is the director?

What happens to our freedom if we accept this reasoning?

I know O Lord, that a human's road is not one's own to choose, that man as he walks, cannot direct his own steps.

(Jeremiah 10:23)

According to this text, why can't humans direct their own steps? Do you agree?

_____

_____

_____

The prophet Jeremiah, in good company with other prophets, as well as the author of Psalms, feels that God chooses the paths that we walk. When cries of injustice are heard, this reminder is often brought forth. This is also cited as justification when the Children of Israel have erred in their ways. Although they have done wrong, the prophet reminds God that in the end it is God who has absolute power over all human behavior. This is not an excuse for wrong behavior, it is an escape clause for God's anger, giving God a reason to bear with the people throughout the good and the bad. This is similar to the language of Job; Job suffered greatly from mishaps, woes, misery and misfortune, but never faltered in his faith, and conceded God's absolute power in their final conversation together.

וַיַּעַן אִיּוֹב אֶת־יְהֹוָה וַיֹּאמַר: בּ יָדַעְתִּ [יָדַעְתִּי] כִּי־כֹל תּוּכָל וְלֹא־יִבָּצֵר מִמְּךָ מְזִמָּה:

Job said in reply to God: I know that You can do everything, that nothing you propose is impossible for You. *(Job 42:1-2)*

Have you ever felt your path has taken turns that were not yours to choose? Explain. Can you remember what that felt like? Where did you feel God was in this journey?

_____
_____
_____

אין אדם נוגע במוכן לחבירו,

No man can touch that which has been prepared in advance for his friend. *(Babylonian Talmud, Yoma 38b)*

ואמר ר חנינא: אין אדם נוקף אצבעו מלמטה אלא א כ
מכריזין עליו מלמעלה, שנאמר: (תהלים ל ז) מה מצעדי גבר כוננו,
(משלי כ) ואדם מה יבין דרכו.

No man bruises his finger here on earth unless it was so decreed in heaven. *(Babylonian Talmud, Hullin 7b)*

What is the implication of these sources on your understanding of your personal destiny?

_____
_____
_____

Comfort can be found in thinking about the world as under the complete surveillance and control of God. There is a lessening of the burden of responsibility when we are able to say that the ultimate responsibility is in God's hands. On the other hand, we know that our creation with two inclinations was a creation to allow us to make choices. We also know that the difference between humanity and God is that we are fallible; we will make bad and wrong choices. In order to do so there must be some free will in the world we occupy.

Rambam (Moses ben Maimon--also known as Maimonides)
(1135-1204 C.E.) A rabbinic authority of Spanish birth, codifier, philosopher, and royal physician. Spent years writing the Mishneh Torah, a codification of the Oral Law which presents the laws of the Torah with Rambam's understanding of the literature written by the Rabbis in Talmudic times.

Saadya Gaon
(882-942 C.E.) Greatest scholar and author of the Geonic period and important leader of Babylonian Jewry. Wrote extensively about philosophy and tried to find rational basis for Torah Law.

Look to the Sources
Compare the words of the Rambam with the idea of free will that is presented by Saadya Gaon:

Maimonides, Mishneh Torah
Free will is bestowed on every human being. If a person desires to turn towards the good path and be just, a person has the power to do so. If a person wishes to turn towards the evil path and be wicked, a person is at liberty to do so… there is no other kind like a person as regards this subject of being able of one's own accord, by reason and thought, to know what is good and what is evil, with none to prevent doing either."

Saadya Gaon
Book of Doctrines and Beliefs
If God's knowledge of things were the eternal cause of their existence, they would have existed from eternity, since God's knowledge of them is eternal. We do, however, believe that God knows things as they exist in reality, i.e. of those things which God creates, God knows in advance that He is going to create them, and of those things which are subject to man's free will, He knows in advance that man is going to choose them. Should one object, "If God knows that a certain person will speak, is it possible for that person to be silent?" We answer quite simply that if that person was to keep silent instead of speaking we should have said in our original statement that God knew that this man would be silent, and we were not entitled to state that God knew that this person would speak. For God knows man's ultimate action such as it will be whether sooner or later after all his planning.
(*"Providence and Free Will"*)

What kind of role does God play in each statement? What is God's power?

Rambam

_____
_____
_____

Saadya

_____
_____
_____

What is the meaning of free will in each statement?

Rambam

_____
_____
_____

Saadya

_____
_____
_____

Both Rambam and Saadya struggle to preserve the idea of free will while acknowledging God's absolute power and knowledge in this world. According to both philosophers, God does not mold our lives or our destinies. We are created with absolute liberty and that is the freedom to choose evil, to become wicked. That is what makes us humans and sets us apart from all other beings. We are not shaped and molded in accordance with someone else's will. We determine our fate, we control our lives, we set the course for our destiny. God might be detached from the process, as God is in the Rambam's thinking, or God might have intimate knowledge of decisions we make before we make them, as we find with Saadya. In both instances what is primary is the free will of humanity to think, and to do, as they wish.

MITZVOT—CHOICE OR OBLIGATION?

(ד) הוא היה אומר עשה רצונו כרצונך. כדי שיעשה רצונך
כרצונו. בטל רצונך מפני רצונו. כדי שיבטל רצון אחרים מפני
רצונך

Rabban Gamliel used to say: Do God's will as though it were your will, so that God will carry out your will as if it were God's will. And nullify your will before God's will, so that God will annul the will of others before your will.   *(Pirkei Avot 2:4)*

The tension between free will and the world of *mitzvot* is only a real tension if you do not believe that you have the freedom to choose to accept being commanded. If you have accepted being a part of the system of *mitzvot*, in doing so you are exercising your free will. The *mishnah* in *Pirkei Avot* adds to this freedom by stating that it is a reciprocal relationship. When you do God's will, then God also chooses to carry out your will. The message of this text is powerful. When we exercise our free will to follow God's path, then God is forced to adapt God's will to our own. In other words, God's will becomes limited when we make the right choices. It is a powerful compulsion to make the 'right' choices.

Can you think of examples that illustrate the idea that if you do God's will as your own, then God will carry our your will as if it were God's?

_____
_____
_____

We do not know the extent of our own power to change and to effect change. But we must act; that is in our power. We have to do our part and we have to hope that God is indeed attentive.
(Rabbi Barukh Bokser, sermon Rosh HaShanah 1989)

Do you believe that you have the freedom to make choices in your religious life? Why or why not?

_____
_____
_____

What do you view as your guidelines in making these choices?

_____
_____
_____

Can your choices have an impact on God's choices in the world? Explain.

_____
_____
_____

We are the children of the modern world, free to believe or disbelieve, to accept or reject, a glorious freedom. (Milton Steinberg)

רבי נחוניא בן הקנה אומר כל המקבל עליו
עול תורה. מעבירין ממנו עול מלכות
ועול דרך ארץ. וכל הפורק ממנו עול תורה.
נותנין עליו עול מלכותועול דרך ארץ

Rabbi Nehunia ben Ha-kana taught: Whoever accepts the yoke of Torah will be spared the burdens of citizenship and of earning a livelihood; but whoever throws off the yoke of Torah will have to bear the burdens of citizenship and of earning a livelihood.
(Pirkei Avot 3:6) [*Citizenship=yoke of kingdom*]

What is the expressed freedom of the individual in this source?

_____
_____
_____

For you, what could be the benefit to following a life of Torah?

_____
_____
_____

The principle of Conservative *halakha* is that in fulfilling *mitzvot* we are walking in the path of God. Living according to these *mitzvot* allows the unfolding of the divine within us. Fulfillment of *mitzvot* is our free submission to God's will, which brings with it an elevation of our humanity.

לְמַעַן תִּזְכְּרוּ
וַעֲשִׂיתֶם אֶת־כָּל־מִצְוֹתָי וִהְיִיתֶם קְדֹשִׁים לֵאלֹהֵיכֶם. מאאֲנִ֞י
יְהוָה אֱלֹהֵיכֶם אֲשֶׁר הוֹצֵאתִי אֶתְכֶם מֵאֶרֶץ מִצְרַיִם לִהְיוֹת
לָכֶם לֵאלֹהִים אֲנִי יְהוָה אֱלֹהֵיכֶם.

"It is for you to remember and do all my commandments and be holy for your God. I am Adonai your God who brought you out of the Land of Egypt to be your God; I am Adonai your God."
(Numbers 16:40-41)

In the third paragraph of the *Shma* we recall the relationship between free will and the world of *mitzvot*. God has given us the free will to make choices in this world. God has also created a system within which we can exercise this free will to make appropriate choices. The hope expressed in the third paragraph of the *Shma* is that we will listen to the choices given to us by God, and choose to follow God's will. Once we have committed ourselves to this path, we are a part of a system that is to be considered a package. *Mitzvot*, ritual, liturgy, are all a part of this journey upon which we have chosen to embark. We continue to exercise our freedom on this path, but it is a freedom that is guided by the rules of the system.

TFILLAH—KEVA OR KAVANAH?
Personal Freedom in Prayer

There is one time in the Jewish year when our thoughts and feelings on personal freedom are most fragile, and that is during the season of the Yamim Noraim (the High Holidays). During these days, as we evaluate our lives, and our behavior, we turn to God and acknowledge our lack of control over our lives and our destiny.

Kavanah
Conscous thought, intention, concentration

Keva
Fixed or precise

> *"As clay in the hand of the potter, to be thickened*
> *or thinned as he wishes, are we in Your hand.*
> *Preserve us with Your love.*
> *Your covenant recall, and not our imperfection.*
> *As stone in the hand of the mason, to be broken*
> *or preserved as he wishes, are we in Your hand,*
> *Master of life and death.*
> *Your covenant recall, and not our imperfection....*
> *As glass in the hand of the glazier, to be melted*
> *or shaped as he wishes, are we in Your hand.*
> *Maintain our fragile balance with Your grace.*
> *Your covenant recall and not our imperfection."*
> *(Mahzor for Rosh HaShanah and Yom Kippur,*
> *The Rabbinical Assembly, p.395)*

How does this piyut express your responsibility to live a moral and Jewish life? Do you feel it provides you ownership over this life?

_____

_____

_____

One of the most moving poetic pieces chanted during the High Holidays, is this *piyut*, *Homer B'Yad HaYotzer*. It likens us humans to clay, glass, stone, materials that an artisan uses in the studio. God is the ultimate artist, molding, shaping, breaking or preserving us. We recognize that this work of art that is our destiny is not ours to determine, and we hope that the partnership between artist and material will enable us to continue to flourish, to mold in our beings the beautiful work of art God has destined us to be. Our hope is that by following the covenant, by realizing and acknowledging our imperfections, the artist will be forgiving. There is no free will in this poem. There is no will; all that we are and all that we will be is shaped by God. It is a passionate and loving God, who wants to produce works of art to be admired in the world, and therein lies our hope and our freedom to continue to be less than perfect beings.

What is the implication of having such a poem woven into the liturgical service of the Yamim Noraim-- High Holy Days?

A similar tension between free will and God's will exists also between the concepts of *Keva* and *Kavanah*. In the following *mishnah* we are taught that prayer should never become staid. One should always have *kavanah*, spiritual intentionality, in one's prayer. However, only a few *mishnayot* later, we read what appears to be a contradictory opinion.

(ד) רבי אליעזר אומר העושה תפלתו קבע. אין תפלתו
תחנונים.

Rabbi Eliezer says: one who makes prayer mechanical, that prayer is not supplication (not heard). *(Mishnah, Brachot 4:4)*

(ה) המתפלל וטעה.
סימן רע לו. ואם שליח צבור הוא. סימן רע לשולחיו. מפני ששלוחו
של אדם כמותו.

When one prays and makes a mistake, that is a bad omen. And if that person be a public leader of prayer it is a bad omen for the community. *(Mishnah, Brachot 5:5)*

What do these mishnayot say about keva and kavanah and their relative importance?

_____

_____

_____

According to these two mishnayot, are you supposed to be precise (keva), in your prayer or are you supposed to forgo precision for a higher level of spiritual intention (kavanah)?

_____

_____

_____

What exactly is a Jew supposed to do? If we are expected to pray with the highest level of *kavanah*, then it is not difficult to assume that there will be times when we will make a mistake in our prayers. It is easy to imagine being swept away by emotions, altering or changing our prayers to fit our mood, or simply skipping a passage with unintentional zest.

What is your freedom in prayer? Is it the freedom to choose to be a part of a Jewish community or the freedom of engaging in conversation with God? Are the two inclusive or exclusive of one another?

According to the first *mishnah*, being swept away by emotions is acceptable, in fact embraced as an expression of our *kavanah*. The second mishnah teaches us that in fact this is not allowable. Mistakes are not only frowned upon, but they can bring bad things, not only to the individual but also to the community for whom this individual was leading the prayers. One *mishnah* opens our freedom of expression, one *mishnah* limits this freedom. We must pray with *kavanah*, but the prayers that we recite must be those of our keva, must be the precise words in their precise order that was determined by the sages, determined within a specific framework of Judaism.

Is it possible for you to engage in prayer of kavanah within the context of keva?

_____

_____

PARADOX OF FAITH AND FREEDOM

Reflection: Is there set destiny to every individual?

Does God imprint our future when we are born?

Do we have any choice in determining the path our lives will take?

הכל צפוי. והרשות נתונה.
All is foreseen, and yet the freedom is granted.
(*Pirkei Avot* 3:15)

God knows all. God foresees all that will ever happen in the world. Despite that foresight, freedom is given by God to all humanity to do as they wish. That is one way of defining free will.

There is an inherent tension in this statement. If God knows all that will ever happen in the world, how is it possible to claim that humans have the free will to do what they choose? Isn't the implication of the text that God already foresees what each person is about to do? What then is 'free' about this will? These questions return us again to the statements of Saadya Gaon and Rambam about the tension between God's will and free will.

How can God's imprint on our life and our freedom to choose coexist?

_____
_____
_____

דדריש ר חנינא בר פפא: אותו מלאך הממונה על ההריון
לילה שמו, ונוטל טפה ומעמידה לפני הקב ה, ואומר לפניו: רבש ע,
טפה זו מה תהא עליה? גבור או חלש, חכם או טיפש, עשיר או עני?
ואילו רשע או צדיק - לא קאמר, כדר חנינא דא ר חנינא: הכל
בידי שמים - חוץ מיראת שמים

As was told in the name of Rabbi Haninah bar Papa: the angel who is responsible for births is called Layla (night), and he takes the drop (of potential life) and presents it to God, and says before him, "Ribono, (Creator) Almighty One, this drop, what will be of it? Will it be heroic, or weak, wise or foolish, rich or poor, righteous or wicked?" This is not as was said in the name of Haninah: "All is in the hands of heaven, except for the fear of heaven." *(Niddah 16b)*

Do either of the statements in the text portray humans as truly free?

In this rich Talmudic tradition two seemingly contradictory positions are recorded and preserved in the text. In the first position our fates are predetermined. The angel *Layla* has a conversation with God asking what traits to record for the unborn fetus. In the second position a contradictory idea is set forth, whereby there is nothing predestined in life except for one trait, the fear, or possibly faith, in God.

Which position in the text do you think attributes a higher level of freedom on us as individuals?

_____
_____
_____

There can be tremendous comfort found in the first illustration. It is a loving image. The tiny little drop, cradled in the hand of a dark angel. The angel approaching God, lovingly asking to bestow traits on the unborn. The possibilities are endless. The tension of the midrash is apparent, for there is no rhyme or rhythm for allocating one set of traits on one person, and a startlingly different set of traits on another. The arbitrary assignment can provide security; after all, this is how God meant for life to be, so why fight it.

The second position is much broader. There is no ascribed attribute to any individual. The implication is that whoever we are, whomever we turn out to be, is entirely in our own hands. We own our destiny. What then is the role of God in this scenario? God implants in each of us the fear of God. This faith, this inherent knowledge of Godliness, forces us to examine our lives, and our choices through a particular lens. Even when we reject this lens, we are still aware that we are choosing to ignore a God–given guideline. This second statement places much more responsibility in our hands for our own destinies:

> Rabbi Yehuda bar Simon said: While the first human lay an unformed mass before the One who spoke and the world came to be, God showed the human every generation and its interpreters; every generation and its sages; every generation and its scribes; every generation and its leaders. (Genesis Rabbah)

Have you ever sat with relatives, looking at photos or hearing stories of ancestors and their accomplishments? How do you feel about your heritage as those stories are being told? Are you affected by these stories?

This text is another illustration of God's imprint on our lives coexisting with our freedom to choose the path our life takes. In this descriptive source, God took the unformed mass of humanity and sat it before a large-screen TV, on which were projected the generations of scholars that would unfold in Jewish history. This would have been an endless parading of individuals who chose the path of Torah as their path in life. In this source God is planting the seeds of desire for Torah in the yet to be created human who would be the first in this lineage. As descendants of this first human our freedom to make choices in impacted by this innate knowledge of the beauty of the lineage of scholars in every generation.

To man is given the freedom to chart his path in life, and he is responsible for the choice he makes. If man were bereft of such freedom of choice, righteousness and wrong, good and evil would have no essential meaning and morality would be an empty phrase. (Morris Adler)

As Conservative Jews how do we express our freedom?

1) **Revelation:**

We believe in God's revelation to us at Mount Sinai and in God's continuing revelation to us through study of Jewish text and through our lives as Jews.

2) *Halakha*

a. Jewish law is indispensable to what it means to be a Jew for theological, communal, and moral reasons.

b. Change in *Halakha* is not done for its own sake, or out of disregard for the law; on the contrary, when rabbis change Jewish law, they do so to enable it to respond to the needs and circumstances of the times and to embody new ethical insights and goals.

Emet Ve-Emunah: Statement of Principles of Conservative Judaism

Revelation—The moment at Mount Sinai when God *revealed* the words of the Torah to the Jewish people.

Halakha—A system of Jewish law stemming from Rabbinical discourse (whether Talmudic or modern).

What are the implications of these two select statements from *Emet Ve-Emunah* on your understanding of the position of Conservative Judaism regarding freedom/ choice?

_____
_____
_____
_____
_____

As Conservative Jews, we take our place proudly in the lineage of scholars of the Torah imprinted in the first human. While we understand that there are important moral compulsions that guide our choices in this world, we see our freedom as being contained within the rubric of *halakha*. Conservative Jews recognize the moment of Sinai as a moment of revelation for all Jews; we have freely become a part of God's people, and have freely accepted the world of Torah, the world of Jewish law as our system in living life. We acknowledge that as humans we can make wrong choices, and within that ability to follow the wrong path, or the right path, is the celebration of our God–given freedom. We welcome this God–given freedom as we critically examine our *halakhic* lives in light of changing realities of our times. It is in this way that as Conservative Jews we live the life walking the paradox of faith and freedom.

The mandate is deceptively simple: Imitateo Deo. Imitate what God did for us and do it for others. How do we imitate God? By relieving suffering. By helping to free the oppressed. By undertaking the ritual of empathy and the search for justice as commitments of our own. Thus does the theology of hope inspire the politics of change. (Letty Cotttin Pogrebin)

Section Four: Rights and Responsibilities of Freedom

In the hour when the Holy One, blessed be He, created the first human, He took him and let him pass before all the trees of the garden of Eden and said to him:

See my works, how fine and excellent they are!
Now all that I have created for you have I created
Think upon this, and do not corrupt and desolate my world
for if you corrupt it, there is no one to set it right after you.

(Ecclessiastes Rabbah)

Our rights and responsibilities to guarantee freedom in this world are a charge from God. We are charged by God to uphold the world God created. That creation is not only the natural world surrounding us, but also the world of humanity with all its complications. We must ensure that the world we leave is less corrupt than the world we first encounter.

צֶדֶק צֶדֶק תִּרְדֹּף לְמַעַן תִּחְיֶה וְיָרַשְׁתָּ אֶת־הָאָרֶץ אֲשֶׁר־יְהוָה אֱלֹהֶיךָ נ־תֵן לָךְ

Justice justice you shall pursue, that you may thrive and occupy the land that the Adonai your God is giving you. (Deuteronomy 16:20)

Central to the gift of freedom that we experience in our lives is the responsibility to uphold freedom not only for ourselves, but for all humans. The pursuit of justice is one that goes across time and space. In every generation throughout the world as Jews we must guarantee freedom. In this section we will examine the rights and responsibilities that come with upholding freedom for communities and individuals within these communities. Looking back on the first section, we will use the statements of: Freedom of, Freedom to, and Freedom from when examining each of these issues. In some cases the freedom of the individual appears limited to safeguard the freedom of the community. In other situations the freedom of the individual takes precedence. There will be situations where there is an intersection of the freedom of the individual and the community. In other cases there are still emerging issues of freedom that are being encountered.

SOCIETAL FREEDOMS

When an individual's act impacts on everyone in a community, then the arena of societal freedoms has been entered. While it would appear that we are each free to do whatever we choose, at any given time, the following story illustrates how this impact can be fatal. In such circumstances, the individual is limited in the ability to exercise this freedom.

> Two men were sitting in a boat, floating away on calm seas. The day was a bright sunny one. The two men were enjoying the peaceful rhythm of water splashing against the side of the boat. It was very lulling. All of a sudden one of the men noticed that the other was very busy with something underneath his seat. Overcome with curiosity, he inquired of his friend what he was doing. His friend replied quietly that he was digging a hole under his seat. The man was horrified! "How could you do that?" he cried out, "The boat will fill with water!" His friend looked at him in astonishment. What right does his friend have to tell him what do on his side of the boat, under his very own seat? The man looked baffled at his friend and stated the obvious, "If you dig a hole under your own seat, do you truly believe that only your side of the boat will fill with water?"

In this amusing illustration, it is obvious to all that, although in theory anyone can cut a hole in their own property, in this particular case when the consequences have fatal impact on others, this freedom is limited. In other situations it is the words or the beliefs of an individual that are limited or expanded to protect the freedom of belief of the larger community.

FREEDOM OF DEFENSE

One of the basic guarantees that we expect in our communities is the freedom to be safe. Is it possible to guarantee freedom while limiting the individual's ability to defend themselves? That is at the core of the issue of gun control in the United States. However, that question is not a new one. The story on the following page from our tradition illustrates the tension between the individual's freedom and communal freedom.

In many Talmudic texts there are often two opinions or more preserved in the text. In many of the stories there are no indications which opinion should be followed. There are some rules of thumb. For example, the opinion of the majority takes precedence over the opinion of only one individual. There are sources that do indicate which opinion is followed. In the source that follows, the text teaches us that the opinion of Rabbi Akiva is followed for law. Despite that, the source preserves both opinions. Primary in Talmudic material is the teaching of methods of argumentation. This teaching style can be more important than the actual bottom line implication of what the law is.

Does your life come first?

שנים שהיו מהלכין בדרך, וביד אחד
מהן קיתון של מים, אם שותין שניהם
- מתים, ואם שותה אחד מהן - מגיע ליישוב. דרש בן פטורא: מוטב
שישתו שניהם וימותו, ואל יראה אחד מהם במיתתו של חבירו.

Two people were on the road, and in the hand of one of them a canteen of water. If they both drink, they both die. If only one of them drinks, that person will reach civilization. Ben Petora taught: Better they should both drink and die, rather than one of them witness the death of the other.

Do you agree with the view taught in the name of Ben Petura that it is better they should both drink and potentially die?

_____

_____

_____

How does this opinion reflect the tension between the freedom of the individual and the community?

_____

_____

_____

עד שבא רבי עקיבא ולימד: וחי אחיך עמך
- חייך קודמים לחיי חבירך.

(This was the opinion held) until Rabbi Akiva came and taught: "And your brother lived with you," this teaches us that your life comes before the life of your friend. (Babylonian Talmud, Baba Metzia 62a)

How does the opinion of Rabbi Akiva differ from that of Ben Petora?

_____

_____

_____

In this source, there is a legitimate understanding that one should try to save oneself and the other person with you. This sense of selflessness is permissible, and even promoted in the words of Ben Petora. On the other hand, according to Rabbi Akiva, it is more important to exercise one's own freedom with self-preservation. The way that the Talmud presents this text demonstrates that while the opinion of Ben Petura might be understandable, the opinion of Rabbi Akiva is preferred. We learn that from the language used in teaching Rabbi Akiva's opinion, "until Rabbi Akiva came and taught…"; at the point of teaching, this opinion was upheld.

Is this position compatible with the sense of freedom of an individual in our communities today?

_____

_____

_____

Can you identify modern scenarios in which you might be called upon to save yourself before saving another person's life?

_____

_____

_____

When does your life take precedence over someone else's life?

מכאן אמרו חכמים בא להורגך השכם להרגו

> From this it is said: when one gets up to attack you, rise early and pre-empt the person with a counter attack. (Tanhuma, Bamidbar 4)

How does this text echo in the opinion of Rabbi Akiva that we encountered on the previous page?

_____

_____

_____

This classic text about self-defense can also be examined through the lens of freedom of the individual and freedom of the community. It is the ultimate act of self-preservation and the ultimate act of exercising one's personal freedom, to pre-empt and attack with a counter attack. However, there are many that will argue that this position violates the rights and the freedom of the community. It can be argued that this position of self-defense is actually a threat to a free society, and should therefore be disregarded.

Describe a situation where this text would serve as a guideline for an individual preserving her/his freedom:

_____

_____

_____

Describe a situation where depending on this text could violate the freedoms of the community:

_____

_____

_____

לֹא תִרְצָח
"You shall not murder" *(Exodus 20:13)*

Is there a contradiction between the commandment to not murder and the permission for self defense?

_____

_____

_____

Although we read very clearly that we are not to murder another person, our Jewish tradition distinguishes between outright killing and self defense. There is recognition that under particular circumstances it becomes necessary to stand up for oneself, even if that entails taking someone else's life.

When does someone else's life take precedence over your own life?

כי ההוא דאתא לקמיה דרבא, אמר ליה: מרי דוראי אמר לי
זיל קטליה לפלניא, ואי לא - קטלינא לך.

It is told about one person who came before Rava with a problem. He said, "the local ruler has ordered me to kill another person, or I will be killed, what do I do?"

Based on the text we have seen so far, what would your answer be for this person?

_____

_____

_____

אמר ליה: ליקטלוך ולא
תיקטול. מאי חזית דדמא דידך סומק טפי? דילמא דמא דההוא גברא
סומק טפי?

Rava ruled that this man may not kill the other person in order to save his own life, stating, "how do you know that your blood is redder than his is? Perhaps the other man's blood is redder?"
(Babylonian Talmud, Pesachim 25b)

What is Rava's basis for his reasoning? Do you agree with him?

_____

_____

_____

Rava reduces the question of whose life comes first to a simple equation. Because Since we are mere mortals and do not know the true worth of another person's life, therefore we must assume at all times that his or her life is more valuable than ours. Although we might want to exercise our freedom of being by defending our life, we learn that to preserve freedom for all individuals we must sacrifice our life.

The obligation to protect other people's lives

"And every obstacle that is also a safety hazard, it is a positive commandment to remove it and beware of it, and be cautious in all ways relating to it, as it says, 'beware for yourself, and preserve your soul.' And if it was not removed, and was left, the obstacles bring about a danger, the positive commandment was violated, and the person is guilty of 'Do not put bloods' [i.e. hazards]"

(Shulkhan Aruch, Hoshen Mishpat 427:8)

What does it mean that it is a *mitzvat aseh*, (a positive commandment) to remove all safety hazards?

_____

_____

_____

According to this *halakha* it is the responsibility of each individual to safeguard the community. One is not only obligated to remove these safety hazards, but even the manner of removal is a part of this obligation. You are expected to remove the safety hazard, because it is considered an obstacle to the community. If you don't remove it, then you are liable if someone is injured.

> **EXERCISE: Name some hazards or obstacles in your community and suggest ways of removing them:**
>
> | HAZARD | REMEDY |
> |---|---|
> | _____ | _____ |
> | _____ | _____ |
> | _____ | _____ |
> | _____ | _____ |
>
> The individual is further cautioned in this halakha that lack of action, is not considered inaction, it is actually considered a violation of *a positive commandment.*
>
> **Go back to the above list and add the danger that inaction would bring in each instance and what would the consequence of failing to act be?**
>
> | CONSEQUENCE | DANGER OF INACTION |
> |---|---|
> | _____ | _____ |
> | _____ | _____ |
> | _____ | _____ |
> | _____ | _____ |

This precept was illustrated most poignantly during the Holocaust. Story after story is told of individuals who were forced by Nazis to choose between being killed or having a child, spouse or parent shot before their eyes. Some made a choice to live, other chose to die.

Can you imagine what it must have felt like to have to make such a choice?

There are times when it is possible to view inaction as merely not doing anything. There are other times when inaction is considered an active choice. In this instance, the inaction is considered a decision to allow danger to lurk in the midst of the community, and this is considered such a hazard that one is guilty of harming another person.

רבי נתן אומר: מניין שלא יגדל אדם כלב רע בתוך ביתו,
ואל יעמיד סולם רעוע בתוך ביתו? ת ל: (דברים כ ב) לא תשים
דמים בביתך.

> Rabbi Natan said: From where do we learn that a person should not raise a vicous dog in the house, and should not stand a rickety ladder in the yard? From what is written: You shall not put bloods [i.e. hazards] in your home. *(Babylonian Talmud, Baba Kamma, 15b)*

This text is an illustration of the perspective that one is forbidden from keeping potential dangers, even in one's own house. This seems to be a clear violation of personal freedom. The arguments repeatedly dwell on the fact that one's personal freedom is limited when there is potential that exercise of this freedom could bring harm to others.

How would you apply these texts to issues in your own communities such as:

Recycling Laws
Right to bear arms vs. gun control
Building codes
Legality of smoking cigarettes
Automobile inspections

Others:

_____
_____
_____

There is no parallel in Canada to the Second Amendment of the American Constitution. The "right to bear arms" did not play a significant role, in Britain or Canada, when Canada was formed; nor has it been part of the debates leading up to the enactment of the Canadian Bill of Rights or the Charter of Rights and Freedoms.

United States Second Amendment: Ratified December 15, 1791

> A well-regulated militia, being necessary to the security of a free state, the right of the people to keep and bear arms, shall not be infringed.

What is the relationship between the United States Amendment guaranteeing freedom to bear arms, and the positive commandment to remove all safety hazards from a community?

_____
_____
_____

A Call to Action: THE SECOND AMENDMENT

The Second Amendment to the United States Constitution states: "A well regulated militia, being necessary to the security of a free State, the right of the people to keep and bear arms, shall not be fringed." These words have been subject to seemingly endless debate on the part of legal scholars, historians, and groups on both sides of the gun control issue in the United States. The argument centers around the question of whether the Second Amendment referred to a *collective* right possessed by states to form armed militias to protect citizens from a tyrannical federal government or whether it guaranteed that all Americans had the right to own guns for their own protection.

On average 12 children are shot and killed by guns each day in the United States of America. Our children deserve to feel safe, to be safe, but they are becoming less safe with so many guns and so few rules. Arguing against gun control is the NRA, with three million members. Despite these public wars, polls indicate the public is supportive of child-safety locks, licensing and background checks for buyers at gun shows.

The primary issues of gun control are legislation of limitations such as closing the gun show loophole (which would not allow people to sell guns at a gun show without a two week waiting period to allow for a safety check), banning high capacity ammunition clips for semi-automatic weapons, having a sensible cooling-off period and background checks, and child-safety locks.

The federal government's statistic is that there is a loaded gun stored unlocked in one out of 11 U.S. households that have both children and firearms.

There are more restrictions in the United States today on children's pajamas and teddy bears than there are on guns. To drive a car you need a license, to take a test, and to be registered and insured. To own a gun you don't have even half of these restrictions.

The population of the U.S. recently climbed to about 273 million people. Given the fact that there are 250 million guns in America, that's about one gun for every one of us over the age of five. As for those under the age of five, according to the Center for Disease Control and Prevention, and the National Center for Health Statistics, there were 84 gun deaths of children under the age of five in 1997. **Where is their freedom to grow up?**

Think About This:

There is a prowler on the loose in your suburban community. The prowler has been known not only to break into homes to steal items, but also to terrorize the residents of the home. Local police have tried to increase their patrol hours, however, it is a small force, and there are not nearly enough personnel to cover the entire community. You have three children at home, and your spouse is often away on business trips. A local member of the community, for whom you have a high degree of respect, has approached you with an offer—purchase a handgun to keep at home, 'just in case.' You are terrified for the welfare of your family. **What do you do?**

1. **Do you buy the gun to protect yourself from the immediate danger? Explain your decision.**
2. **What risks did you consider?**
3. **If you chose to buy the gun, what, if any, precautions should you take?**
4. **Are there other alternatives to buying a gun?**
5. **How can you fulfill the commandment to remove obstacles while still protecting your family?**
6. **Are there other alternatives?**

Freedom of defense is freedom to

_____

Freedom of defense is freedom of

_____

Freedom of defense is freedom from

_____

A Call to Action—STATEMENT FROM THE CHILDREN'S DEFENSE FUND

Statement by Marian Wright Edelman, Founder and President of the Children's Defense Fund on the School Shooting in Mount Morris Township, Michigan.

WASHINGTON, D.C — How many more children have to die before we say enough is enough? Once again we are faced with the horror of still another child killing a child. If children aren't safe in their first grade classroom, where is their safe harbor? How young do the victims have to be before we stop the proliferation of guns in our nation? According to the latest statistics, 191 children under ten were killed by gunfire in 1997; 84 of them were under five. More preschool children were killed in one year by guns than police killed in the line of duty. America has had more wake-up calls than any decent nation should tolerate.

There are two victims in this case—the little girl who has lost her life and the young shooter who, authorities now tell us, was a victim of this nation's romance with guns. As often happens, we can trace still another tragic child death to adult irresponsibility. Everyone is asking how a six-year-old could get a gun. The answer lies with adults. Adults who made the gun, who sold the gun, who bought the gun, who stole the gun, who left the gun loaded and unlocked so a six-year-old could take the life of another and irrevocably change his own life and the lives of those left to mourn. Adults glorify gun use in our nation—in the movies, on television, on the Internet—without regard to its ef-

fect on many of our children who cannot distinguish between what's real and what's not.

We must do more to stop this senseless violence. We can't just talk about it and then do nothing until the next shooting when we will profess shock again. We must act now to get to the root causes of the problem: the easy availability of guns to too many of our children; the manufacturing and selling of non-sporting firearms; the absence of effective gun control measures including licensing; the lack of parental responsibility and moral example of guidance about the need for respect for life; the absence of hope among young people who see violence as the way to solve disputes and an epidemic of family and media violence that leave children thinking violence is the way to solve problems.

This latest tragedy is no fluke. It is a senseless, immoral neglect of all of us as a nation to fail to protect children instead of guns—and to speak out against the pervasive culture of violence. We don't have a child problem in America—we have an adult problem. Adult hypocrisy got us here, it is now up to responsible adults to take a range of concrete steps to stop these preventable child tragedies.

For more information: Contact Gigi Hinton at (202) 662-3619   www.cdf.org

FREEDOM OF RELIGION

Religious freedom is a value that we all consider inherent to modern societies. On the other hand, as a Jewish people we also have a learned religious consciousness as the "Chosen" people. There is a possible tension between the value of religious freedom and the Jewish sense of chosenness.

Is religious freedom compatible with Jewish beliefs?

_____

_____

_____

Do you feel that you have complete freedom to practice Judaism?

_____

_____

_____

ALEINU

"We rise to our duty to praise the Adonai of all, to acclaim the creator. Who made our lot unlike that of other people, assigning to us a unique destiny... and so we hope in

עָלֵינוּ לְשַׁבֵּחַ לַאֲדוֹן הַכֹּל, לָתֵת גְּדֻלָּה לְיוֹצֵר בְּרֵאשִׁית, שֶׁלֹּא עָשָׂנוּ כְּגוֹיֵי הָאֲרָצוֹת וְלֹא שָׂמָנוּ כְּמִשְׁפְּחוֹת הָאֲדָמָה, שֶׁלֹּא שָׂם חֶלְקֵנוּ כָּהֶם וְגוֹרָלֵנוּ כְּכָל־הֲמוֹנָם. וַאֲנַחְנוּ כּוֹרְעִים וּמִשְׁתַּחֲוִים וּמוֹדִים לִפְנֵי מֶלֶךְ מַלְכֵי הַמְּלָכִים הַקָּדוֹשׁ בָּרוּךְ הוּא, שֶׁהוּא נוֹטֶה שָׁמַיִם וְיוֹסֵד אָרֶץ, וּמוֹשַׁב יְקָרוֹ בַּשָּׁמַיִם מִמַּעַל וּשְׁכִינַת עֻזּוֹ בְּגָבְהֵי מְרוֹמִים. הוּא אֱלֹהֵינוּ, אֵין עוֹד. אֱמֶת מַלְכֵּנוּ, אֶפֶס זוּלָתוֹ, כַּכָּתוּב בְּתוֹרָתוֹ: וְיָדַעְתָּ הַיּוֹם וַהֲשֵׁבֹתָ אֶל לְבָבֶךָ, כִּי יהוה הוּא הָאֱלֹהִים בַּשָּׁמַיִם מִמַּעַל וְעַל הָאָרֶץ מִתָּחַת, אֵין עוֹד.

You, God, our God, soon to see your splendor, sweeping idolatry away so that false gods will be utterly destroyed, perfecting earth by Your kingship so that all human-kind will invoke your name, bringing all the earth's wicked back to You, repentant. Then all who live will know that to You every knee must bend, every tongue pledge loyalty." (*Siddur Sim Shalom*)

What does the Aleinu claim will happen to those who do not believe in God?

_____

_____

_____

This prayer can be described as one that attacks the people who follow other faiths. It can also be seen as a prayer that describes what happens to their faith or religion, not to them.

What do you think is being described? How does it make you feel as a Jew?

_____

_____

_____

Is this prayer consistent with a belief in freedom of religion? Why or why not?

_____

_____

_____

Historically, one of the more controversial lines of this *tfilla*, 'for they bow down to nothingness', was removed from the recitation of the Aleinu by the Conservative movement. This was one attempt to reconcile the idea of choseness with the idea of religious freedom and pluralism. Nonetheless, the language of the Aleinu implies that in the end of days, in a utopian society, all inhabitants of the world will believe in God. The language of the Aleinu prayer implies that while all people are free to believe in what they wish, they are misled in doing so, and in the end will return to the 'proper' way of belief, which is belief in the Jewish God.

ת ר, שאלו פלוסופין את
הזקנים ברומי: אם אלהיכם אין רצונו בעבודת כוכבים, מפני מה
אינו מבטלה? אמרו להם: אילו לדבר שאין העולם צורך לו היו
עובדין הרי הוא מבטלה, הרי הן עובדין לחמה וללבנה ולכוכבים
ולמזלות, יאבד עולם מפני השוטים? אלא עולם כמנהגו נוהג, ושוטים
שקלקלו עתידין ליתן את הדין.

Certain philosophers once asked the Jewish elders when they were in Rome: 'if your God hates idolatry, why doesn't your God destroy the idols?'. And so God would, the elders replied, if only those objects worshipped were not needed by the world. But you worship the sun, and moon, and stars. Should God destroy the world because of the fools upon it?

(Babylonian Talmud, Avodah Zara 54b)

What is the message in this text? What, if anything, should be our response?

_____

_____

_____

This text echoes the message in the Aleinu prayer that we recite. It seems to call idolatry an objectionable pursuit, and yet, it makes clear why God does not intervene in the existence of this practice. Although the people engaging in this worship are called fools in this text, God will not exercise supreme justice in eliminating such practice.

Another way of reading this text is that God tolerates behaviors that are obviously foolish to God. If God is able to tolerate behavior that is so obviously distasteful to God, who are we as humans to show any less tolerance. We, who cannot know with the same certainty what is or isn't desired by God, should demonstrate even more tolerance, even for those behaviors that appear to us to violate God's will.

Jewish Teachings on Tolerance

If you harm your neighbor a little, let it seem in your eyes as if you harmed him a lot; if you have done much for your neighbor, may it seem like a little; if your neighbor has done a little good for you, may it be regarded as considerable. *(Avot d'Rabbi Natan 41)*

What natural human tendencies does this text come to counteract?

_____

_____

_____

This text is an explanation of how we can learn to demonstrate tolerance towards others. *Avot d'Rabbi Natan* teaches one to always be harsh and judgmental about one's own behavior, but forgiving about someone else's behavior. At all times a person is implored to behave modestly towards others, and to treat others with utmost forgiveness.

How might this text be applied to an understanding of religious freedom?

_____

_____

_____

Jewish Teachings on Religious Freedom

אמר רב יהודה אמר שמואל:
שהקיפו דברים כעכנא זו, וטמאוהו. תנא: באותו היום השיב
רבי אליעזר כל תשובות שבעולם ולא קיבלו הימנו. אמר להם: אם
הלכה כמותי - חרוב זה יוכיח. נעקר חרוב ממקומו מאה אמה, ואמרי
לה: ארבע מאות אמה: אמרו לו: אין מביאין ראיה מן החרוב. חזר
ואמר להם: אם הלכה כמותי - אמת המים יוכיחו. חזרו אמת המים
לאחוריהם. אמרו לו: אין מביאין ראיה מאמת המים. חזר ואמר להם:
אם הלכה כמותי - כותלי בית המדרש יוכיחו. הטו כותלי בית
המדרש ליפול.

"On that day Rabbi Eliezer (disputing the other sages), brought all the proofs in the world, (to support his arguments), but the sages would not accept his proofs. He said to them, "If the law is according to me, let this locust tree prove it." The tree moved a hundred cubits. The sages said to him, "The locust tree cannot prove anything." Then he said to them: "If the law is according to me, let this stream of water prove it." The stream of water turned and flowed backward. They said to him: "The stream cannot prove it." Then he said to them, "If the law is according to me, let the walls of this house of study prove it." The walls of the house of study began to topple.

If you were sitting in this house of study, what would you believe?

_____

_____

_____

The text continues:

גער בהם רבי יהושע, אמר להם: אם תלמידי חכמים
מנצחים זה את זה בהלכה - אתם מה טיבכם? לא נפלו מפני כבודו
של רבי יהושע, ולא זקפו מפני כבודו של רבי אליעזר, ועדין מטין
ועומדין.

Rabbi Yehoshua reprimanded the walls saying, "If scholars are disputing with one another about the law, what business is it of yours?" The walls did not fall down out of respect for Rabbi Yehoshua, but they did not straighten up out of respect for Rabbi Eliezer, and they are still inclined.

I have no need to exalt my people to heaven, to trumpet its superiority above all other nations, in order to find justification for existence. I at least know why I remain a Jew - or rather, I can find no meaning in such a question any more than if I were asked why I remain my father's son. (Achad HaAm, "Slavery in Freedom")

How do you understand the reprimand of Rabbi Yehoshua?

_____

_____

_____

The text concludes:

חזר ואמר להם: אם הלכה כמותי - מן השמים יוכיחו.
יצאתה בת קול ואמרה: מה לכם אצל רבי אליעזר שהלכה כמותו
בכל מקום! עמד רבי יהושע על רגליו ואמר: לא בשמים היא. - מאי
(דברים ל) לא בשמים היא? - אמר רבי ירמיה: שכבר נתנה תורה
מהר סיני, אין אנו משגיחין בבת קול, שכבר כתבת בהר סיני
בתורה (שמות כ ג) אחרי רבים להטת.

Then Rabbi Eliezer said to them: "If the law is according to me, let the heaven prove it."

A *bat kol* came forth and said: "Why do you dispute with Rabbi Eliezer? The law is according to him in every case."

Thereupon Rabbi Yehoshua rose to his feet and said: "It is not in the heavens!"

What does it mean that it is not in heaven? Rabbi Yermiah said: "Torah was already given at Sinai, and so we aren't attentive to the *bat kol*, for in the written Torah at Sinai it was already written to follow the majority."

(Talmud Bavli, Baba Metzia 59b)

Why shouldn't heaven have a say in which way the law should be understood?

_____

_____

_____

It is clear in this text that Rabbi Eliezer understands God's law better than the other Rabbis. His is a more accurate interpretation, and the power of this insight allows inanimate objects to demonstrate their support of his positions. However, stronger than the "correct" interpretation of the law, is the process of legal interpretations that the sages engaged in. This process is as sacred as the actual interpretation of the law. Even the *bat kol*, God's representative voice in heaven, cannot support Rabbi Eliezer's position over the position of the sages. Freedom of religion stems from the natural process of human interpretation of law. This process is held so sacred in our Rabbinic text, that even God cannot intervene.

We might have thought that God dictated how to interpret sacred text, after all the text is God's word. This Talmudic passage clearly illustrates the idea that even when humans interpret the law in a way that is not in accordance with God's intentions, the human interpretation is nonetheless the right one. God no longer has a vote or a veto in how the halakha is interpreted. God has given us the freedom of interpretation and must abide by our understanding of these laws.

This passage from the Babylonian Talmud illustrates one approach of the Rabbis to the idea of where religious authority stems from. If religious authority is human driven, as suggested in this passage, there would be a stronger argument for religious pluralism both within Judaism and amongst different religions.

Can you provide a concrete demonstration of how this text could apply to our understanding of religious freedom?

_____

_____

_____

Does religious freedom mean that anything goes in religion and all must be respected?

_____

_____

_____

Are there any limitations suggested in this text that might also limit how we understand religious freedom?

_____

_____

_____

According to the United States First Amendment, the Canadian Charter of Rights and the Israeli Declaration of Independence, each individual has the right to practice his or her own religion or no religion at all. In the United States, government is prohibited from encouraging or promoting religion in any way. That includes financial support to any religion. Furthermore, the 'free exercise' clause of the First Amendment provides each individual with the right to worship or not worship based on personal choice. There can be no penalty for exercising this right.

In 1971, the Supreme Court of the United States determined in Lemon vs. Kurtzman that there are three tests that determine whether a particular government act or policy unconstitutionally promotes religion. The Lemon Test states that a policy must:

1. Have a non-religious purpose

2. Not end up promoting or favoring any set of religious beliefs

3. Not overly involve the government with religion

EXERCISE: Can you determine whether the following cases hold up under the Lemon test? Why or why not?

1) Your school is interested in establishing a religion track as part of social studies. Because most of your school is not Jewish it has been determined that the school will offer a course on Christian theology. To accommodate the needs of the Jewish students a Rabbi will come in during those class periods to teach Jewish theology to the Jewish students.

_____

_____

_____

2) Your school has had a difficult year. One of the members of the football team was suspended for cheating on a test, and students blame the suspension for the team losing in the playoffs. The result has been distrust between the students and the administration. In an attempt to unify the school and restore faith, it has been suggested that school begin with a moment of silence or prayer. The prayers will not refer to God or Jesus, but to a 'higher being', so that they are non-denominational.

_____

_____

_____

3) Your community wants to include a spiritual element in the graduation ceremonies. The idea is to recognize that this is an important milestone in everyone's lives, and worthy of deeper reflection. In order to include everyone, the suggestion is that each year a different member of clergy from a different religion/denomination be invited to lead the prayer, in order to be inclusive of all students.

_____

_____

_____

Think About This:

You are in a community in Kentucky. For the first time it has been decided to invite you, as a Jewish teenager who is active in your community, to recite the invocation at the opening football game for the local high school. All of your friends will be at the game and they are so excited that you were asked to be the representative. You are not sure you are comfortable with this moment of public prayer.

What do you do? Do you accept the honor and if so, what kind of invocation do you recite? Or, do you decline the invitation and why?

_____

_____

_____

A Call to Action—Separation of Church and State in the United States—*Resolution of the United Synagogue of Conservative Judaism, approved 1997*

WHEREAS, The Courts of the United States have traditionally prevented all attempts to combine Church and State in violation of the First Amendment of the United States Constitution and of the constitutions of the various states; and

WHEREAS, the Religious Right, a broad coalition of politically active fundamentalist Christian leaders, continues to pressure Congress into passing laws that would legislate their brand of 'morality', including the introduction of prayer into the public schools and public funding of religious symbols;

NOW, THEREFORE BE IT RESOLVED that the United Synagogue of Conservative Judaism opposes all forms of organized public prayer, religious exercises or sectarian bible classes in primary and secondary public schools, including 'moments of silence or meditation' by which prayer is expressly or implicitly encouraged or recommended; it being the firm position of the United Synagogue of Conservative Judaism that prayer, religious experiences and religious education are the responsibilities of the home, the synagogue and other places of worship; and

BE IT FURTHER RESOLVED, that the United Synagogue of Conservative Judaism opposes the public funding or display on public grounds of religious symbols which imply support of religious doctrine; and

BE IT FURTHER RESOLVED, that the United Synagogue of Conservative Judaism undertake to inform its affiliated congregations of the importance of the separation of Church and State and asks the members of the congregations to communicate their feelings with the appropriate public officials.

Religious freedom is freedom to

_____

Religious freedom is freedom of

_____

Religious freedom is freedom from

_____

INDIVIDUAL FREEDOMS

Each and every individual has a basic right to freedom. We are all members of societies and there are often times when these freedoms are limited in order to preserve the larger good of the community. In other cases, the limitations of society are not designed to preserve a larger good, but instead are an imposition of the beliefs of the community on the individual. We will examine some political issues that fall in the realm of the individual but are under legislative fire.

REPRODUCTIVE RIGHTS

While the issue of reproductive rights has been a charged one in the public arena, it is for Jews, a political issue of preserving the freedom of an individual to follow his or her personal moral code and religious tradition. Jewish tradition is sensitive to the sanctity of life. Nonetheless there are sanctions for abortion in Jewish law under some circumstances.

Does the fetus have autonomy?

וְכִי־יִנָּצוּ אֲנָשִׁים וְנָגְפוּ אִשָּׁה הָרָה וְיָצְאוּ יְלָדֶיהָ וְלֹא
יִהְיֶה אָסוֹן עָנוֹשׁ יֵעָנֵשׁ כַּאֲשֶׁר יָשִׁית עָלָיו בַּעַל הָאִשָּׁה וְנָתַן
בִּפְלִלִים: כְּגוֹאם־אָסוֹן יִהְיֶה וְנָתַתָּה נֶפֶשׁ תַּחַת נָפֶשׁ:

> When men fight and one of them pushes a pregnant woman and a miscarriage results, but no other damage ensues, the one responsible shall be fined according as the woman's husband may exact from him… but if other damage ensues, the penalty shall be life for life.
>
> *(Exodus 21:22-23)*

What is the importance in the fact that the penalty for a miscarriage is 'only' a monetary fine?

_____

_____

_____

Compare that penalty to the penalty of 'life for life' that is provided for if the mother is injured or killed:

_____

_____

_____

The status of the fetus in this Biblical text is one of developing life. The implication of the monetary fine is that the fetus is not considered a fully formed person, and so there can only be a civil penalty for the miscarriage. That is distinct from the penalty for killing the mother, a crime considered a clear homicide.

Whose life takes precedence?

(ו) האשה שהיא מקשה
לילד.מחתכין את הולד במעיה ומוציאין אותו אברים אברים.מפני
שחייה קודמין לחייו. יצא רובו.אין נוגעין בו.שאין דוחין נפש מפני
נפש:

"If a woman is suffering in hard labor, the child is cut out of her womb, and brought out limb by limb, because her life takes precedence over its life. If its greater part has already come forth, you do not touch it, for one life does not supersede another."

(Mishnah, Ohalot 7:6)

Whose life takes precedence in this *mishnah*?

_____

_____

_____

Based on this *mishnah*, *halakha* permits, and even mandates, abortion in any case where there is danger to the mother's life. The mother's life takes precedence over the life of the unborn fetus up until the moment when a majority of the fetus has emerged.

The mother's life takes precedence over the fetus, in part because the opinion expressed here does not view the fetus as a fully formed life. The fetus is not treated as a fully formed life in this *mishnah* until the majority of the fetus has emerged from the womb. This view differs from other religious opinions that have influenced modern public opinion about abortions.

What is the value of the life of an individual?

Conservative Movement Statement on the Permissibility of Abortion—Committee on Jewish Law and Standards, Adopted 1983

Jewish tradition is sensitive to the sanctity of life, and does not permit abortion on demand. However, it sanctions abortion under some circumstances because it does not regard the fetus as an autonomous person. This is based party on the Bible (Exodus 21:22-23), which prescribes monetary damages when a person injures a pregnant woman, causing a miscarriage. The Mishnah (Ohalot 7:6) explicitly indicates that one is to abort a fetus if the continuation of pregnancy might imperil the life of the mother. Later authorities have differed as to how far we might go in defining the peril to the mother in order to justify abortion.

The Rabbinical Assembly Committee on Jewish Law and Standards takes the view that an abortion is justifiable if a continuation of pregnancy might cause the mother severe physical or psychological harm, or when the fetus is judged by competent medical opinion as severely defective. The fetus is a life in the process of development, and the decision to abort should never be taken lightly. Before reaching her final decision, the mother should consult with the father, other members of her family, her physician, her spiritual leader and any other person who can help her in assessing the many grave legal and moral issues involved.

What does this statement of the Committee on Jewish Law and Standards add to our understanding of when God might permit an abortion?

_____

_____

_____

Rabbinic sources are resounding in their clarity that in the case where a mother's life is in danger, an abortion is mandated. More commentators expand this thought and determine that in the case of physical harm, where there is a chance that the mother's life could be threatened an abortion is permitted. There is more ambiguity in the case of a mother's psychological harm. In the statement of the CJLS the Conservative movement puts forth that a mother's severe psychological harm should be judged as physical harm is judged and that an abortion is permissible and at times mandated.

In many cases, the issues surrounding the pregnancy are not clear cut. It is because abortions are a complex issue that no woman takes lightly, that the CJLS recommends that women consult not only family and physician, but also speak with their spiritual leader before making a decision. The CJLS supports reproductive freedom, though it is concerned with guidelines for specific cases.

In what circumstances, if any, would abortion be permitted or required?

דרור יקרא 73

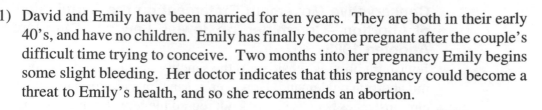

Think About This:

1) David and Emily have been married for ten years. They are both in their early 40's, and have no children. Emily has finally become pregnant after the couple's difficult time trying to conceive. Two months into her pregnancy Emily begins some slight bleeding. Her doctor indicates that this pregnancy could become a threat to Emily's health, and so she recommends an abortion.

Would the CJLS permit an abortion under these circumstances?
Would the CJLS require an abortion under these circumstances?

2) Annie is 16 years old, and has just discovered that she is pregnant. She is completely horrified, particularly because her pregnancy is a result of sexual violence. Annie knows that her parents would support her regardless of her decision. However, Annie is not sure she could love a child born out of this violence, and is not sure if she could accept herself with this pregnancy.

Would the CJLS permit an abortion under these circumstances?
Would the CJLS require an abortion under these circumstances?

A Call to Action—USCJ Resolution on Abortion

The USCJ supports legislation maintaining the legality and accessibility of abortion so that in those cases where our religuos authorities determine that an abortion is warranted halakhically, obtaining that abortion will not be hindered by our civil law.

Reproductive freedom is freedom to _____

Reproductive freedom is freedom of _____

Reproductive freedom is freedom from _____

WHEREAS, Jewish tradition cherishes the sanctity of life, even the potential of life which a pregnant woman carries within her; and
WHEREAS, under certain unfortunate circumstances, such as when the life or the health of the mother are in jeopardy, Judaism sanctions, even mandates, abortion, although Judaism does not condone or permit abortion for contraceptive purposes; and
WHEREAS, Judaism does not believe that personhood and human rights begin with conception (the premise that personhood begins with conception is founded on a religious position which is not identical with Jewish tradition); and
WHEREAS, under special circumstances, Judaism chooses and requires abortion as an act which affirms and protects the life, well-being and health of the mother; and
WHEREAS, to deny a Jewish woman and her family the ability to obtain a safe, legal abortion when so mandated by Jewish tradition, is to deprive Jews of their fundamental right of religious freedom;
NOW, THEREFORE, BE IT RESOLVED that the United Synagogue of Conservative Judaism continues to affirm its strong opposition to any

further weakening, limitation, or withdrawal of the 1973 Supreme Court decision of Roe v. Wade; and
BE IT FURTHER RESOLVED that the United Synagogue of Conservative Judaism, in light of the recent Supreme Court decision and the efforts of the U.S. government to limit the choices available to most Americans, must be diligent in the efforts to safeguard and preserve the full personal and religious freedom given to the American people; and
BE IT FURTHER RESOLVED that the United Synagogue of Conservative Judaism opposes any legislative attempt through constitutional amendments, the deprivation of Medicaid., family services and/or other current welfare services, to weaken the force of the United States Supreme Court's decision permitting choice; and
BE IT FURTHER RESOLVED that the United Synagogue of Conservative Judaism encourages the various provinces of Canada and the Canadian government to preserve the rights of all women to legal abortions.

Resolution of the United Synagogue of Conservative Judaism, passed 1991

FREE SPEECH

It seems that every year there is another challenge to free speech in our community. Often these challenges come from groups such as the Ku Klux Klan, which argue for their right to march on our streets, spreading their hatred. On the one hand, the hatred that is spewed is appalling. On the other hand, limiting the freedom of speech of individuals is not imaginable. Perhaps, today it will be determined that these individuals should not be allowed free speech, but then who is to say that tomorrow someone else won't deem my right to free speech be limited? This tension is not new to our society. Jewish law has long recognized that with the freedom to speak comes the burden to speak responsibly.

The Power of Language

> "Just as it is forbidden to wrong another in buying and selling it is forbidden to wrong a person with words. As it is said, "Do not wrong one another, but fear thy God. (Leviticus 25:17) The reference here is to wronging with words. It is a worse offense to wrong with words than to wrong in buying and selling, for in the one case restitution is possible, in the other impossible; in one case the victim is only cheated out of money, in the other wronged in person."
>
> *(Kitzur Shulkhan Aruch, Chapter 63)*

The Jewish response to wrongdoing is to measure the degree of restitution the offense necessitates. In other words, how much does a given wrongdoing cost the individual owner? In the case of buying and selling, although the action is still wrong, it is a measurable wrong. It is possible to calculate how much the loss of sale or the cheating of money would cost an individual. In the case of words, however, restitution cannot be calculated on a monetary basis. There is no sum of money that can restore personhood.

THE PARABLE OF THE FEATHERS

There was once a person in a town who was spreading evil rumors about another person in the town. All the townspeople had heard these stories, there was no place to hide from them. The grieved person brought this to the attention of the Rabbi. The Rabbi called the gossip culprit to ask about this situation. The gossiper admitted spreading the gossip, but insisted that it would be ok. Repair would happen - by simply spreading the news that the gossip was unfounded. The Rabbi thought about this for a moment and agreed that this would be a good thought. However, as a caveat, the Rabbi asked that the gossiper take a pillow, rip it up, and let the feathers fly into the wind. The Rabbi asked the gossiper to come to the shul, and bring those feathers to the meeting. The very next day the Rabbi sat at the shul awaiting the gossiper. Finally, hours late for the meeting, the gossiper dragged in, with only a handful of feathers. "Are those all the feathers that were in the pillow?" the Rabbi asked in astonishment. Embarrassed, the gossiper looked down and whispered, "No, there were many more feathers. These were all the ones I could gather back." The Rabbi looked down at the gossiper and gently said, "I think you understand that

although it was easy to spread the pillow feathers around the town, that it is nearly impossible to gather them up afterwards. So too of course with gossip. There is no way once you say something about another, for you to ever gather it back."

Can you illustrate this case with a similar personal story?

_____
_____
_____

Have you ever been the victim of *lashon harah*? What were the circumstances?

_____
_____
_____

Have you ever tried to "take back" a rumor once it has been spread?

_____
_____
_____

Do you have an example of *lashon hara* hurting someone's life?

_____
_____
_____

> The person who slanders piles up offenses as high as the sky, and deserves to be stoned.
>
> *(Babylonian Talmud, Arachin 15b)*

Of all transgressions, *lashon hara* is perhaps the easiest to commit. It's result can be potent enough to destroy a person's life. Consequently, in determining a punishment for this transgression the sages equate it with idolatry, incest and even murder. It is doubtful that this equation was meant to be taken literally. It was however, a way of demonstrating the hope that people would avoid committing the crime of slander and gossip.

Responsibility of Free Speech

ארשב ג לטבי עבדיה פוק זבין לי צדו טבא
מן שוקא נפק זבן ליה לישן א ל פוק זבין לי צדו בישא מן שוקא נפק
זבן ליה לישן

Rabban Gamliel commanded his servant Tobi to go to the market and purchase the best that could be had. Tobi returned with a tongue. The following day he sent Tobi out to buy the worst that the market had to offer. Tobi went out, and again returned with tongue.

א ל מהו דין דכד אנא אמר לך צדו טבא את זבן לי
לישן וכד אנא אמר לך צדו בישא את זבן לי לישן א ל מינה טבתא
ומינה בישתא כד הוה טב לית טבה מיניה וכד ביש לית ביש מיניה

When asked why both times he purchased the same item, Tobi replied, "There is nothing better than a good tongue and nothing worse
than an evil one." *(VaYikra Rabbah 33)*

The power of speech, Rabban Gamliel learned from his servant, could be both the
most positive characteristic, or the worst, depending on how it was used. One of our
responsibilities as humans who dwell within a community is to recognize that the
power of free speech is not only a burden to recognize what not to say, but also
should be a sacred task of saying the good that should be stated. Free speech according to the text of *VaYikra Rabbah* is about saying 'please' and 'thank you'.
Free speech is about encouraging people, commending them for their good deeds,
and recognizing their accomplishments.

EXERCISE: Freedom Speech Means That...

Mark the appropriate place for each item below:

	Strongly Disagree					Strongly Agree
I can say whatever I want about anybody	1	2	3	4	5	6
I can say anything I want about people who are in the public eye	1	2	3	4	5	6
There are no ramifications for saying what I think	1	2	3	4	5	6
There are no ramifications for saying whatever I want	1	2	3	4	5	6
If I hurt someone for speaking the truth I am liable	1	2	3	4	5	6
If someone is willing to pay for my information it is my right to sell it	1	2	3	4	5	6
I have to be as responsible about what I am saying about others, as I would want them to be considerate about me	1	2	3	4	5	6
Hate groups can't be stopped their word	1	2	3	4	5	6
There can be no limits on what public school teachers may tell students regarding sex education	1	2	3	4	5	6
People are allowed to distort facts or state half-truths to make a political point.	1	2	3	4	5	6

Celebration of Free Speech

All words are sacred, they reflect the words of God. Everything said in earnest interpretation of the text, in sincere regard of tradition, is part of God's heritage to us. How does this affect the way that we treat a minority opinion? If we know that the person we are disagreeing with is still considered to be speaking words of God, how should we think about our interaction with this person?

This idea that free speech is about the sacredness of our disagreements is best illustrated in the famous disagreements between the two houses of study, Hillel and Shamai. The *Mishnah* has an ongoing record of all the *halakhic* issues that these two individuals and their schools of thought disagreed about. However, regardless of their disagreements, the tradition maintains that there was never a problem for members of one school to eat in the home of a member of another school, or to marry someone from a different school. Free speech is more than peaceful coexistence. Free speech as illustrated here is about merged coexistence.

(יז) כל מחלוקת שהיא
לשם שמים. סופה להתקים. ושאינה לשם שמים. אין סופה להתקים.
איזו היא מחלוקת שהיא לשם שמים. זו מחלוקת הלל ושמאי. ושאינה
לשם שמים. זו מחלוקת קורח וכל עדתו:

Any controversy that is for God's sake, will exist through the end, but any controversy that is not for God's sake, will not exist permanently. Which is a controversy that is for God's sake? That is the controversy of Hillel and Shamai. What is controversy that is not for God's sake? That is the controversy of Korah and his faction (Numbers 16:1).

(Avot 5:17)

What is an example of an argument that is for God's sake?

_____

_____

_____

What is an example of an argument that is not for God's sake?

_____

_____

_____

The guideline put forth in this text is very clear. Argument for personal gain or power is not justifiable. Arguments that are intended to understand God's will in the world, to uncover the sacred within the mundane, to further our religious commitment, is considered a sacred controversy, one that is not only sanctified, but even celebrated in this text. However, this also impacts how we treat one another when engaging in such controversy. The text from *Pirkei Avot* demonstrates that there are disagreements that are sacred. If we can recognize a disagreement as sacred, how then do we treat the individual with whom we have this disagreement? How do we continue to live merged lives with these individuals? *Pirkei Avot* and related texts about the controversies of Hillel and Shamai teach that free speech is a sacred privilege that is for God's sake. Free speech is not an excuse in these traditions for hatred or for dismissal of those with whom we can't agree.

"Without Freedom of Thought, there can be no such Thing as Wisdom; and no such Thing as public Liberty, without Freedom of Speech." (Benjamin Franklin, The New England Courant July 9, 1722)

United States Constitution *The First Amendment:*	Can. Charter of Rights and Freedoms *Section Two: Fundamental Freedoms*
"Congress shall make no law respecting an establishment of religion, or prohibiting the free exercise thereof; or abridging the freedom of speech, or of the press; or the right of the people peaceably to assemble, and to petition the government for a redress of grievances."	Everyone has the following fundamental freedoms: 1. freedom of conscience and religion; 2. freedom of thought, belief, opinion and expression, including freedom of the press and other media of communication; 3. freedom of peaceful assembly; and 4. freedom of association

What similarities do we find between the First Amendment, The Canadian Charter, and the Jewish textual protection of the right to disagree?

_____

_____

_____

Think About This:

An unusual number of students have taken a course with Professor Haran. Each of them has found that there are difficulties with the Professor; grading seems arbitrary, the reading list is beyond the scope of their comprehension, and the written requirements are extensive. The students decide to post notices on the Student Union website, alerting other students to the risk of taking a course with Professor Haran. As a result the registration numbers for Haran's spring course have dropped significantly. The professor asks the University to remove the complaints from the website, stating that it is impossible to properly teach under such conditions. The University concedes. What should the student response to this situation be? Whose rights are being violated in this scenario?

How does our understanding of Jewish tradition reflect on this situation?

_____

_____

_____

What arguments might we develop to support or refute the University's behavior?

_____

_____

_____

Do you agree or disagree with the position that Jewish tradition articulates?

A Call to Action—Settlement Ends Attempt To Punish Student For Web Site in Washington State

FOR IMMEDIATE RELEASE
Friday, April 7, 2000

KENT, WA — A settlement between student Nick Emmett and Kent School District has ended the district's attempt to punish the student because of a Web site created on his home computer. Under terms of the settlement negotiated by the American Civil Liberties Union of Washington State, the suburban Seattle district will not pursue disciplinary action against Emmett over the Web site and will pay his attorney fees.

The agreement comes after one of the first court rulings on student free speech in cyberspace. In February, Chief Judge John Coughenour of the U.S. District Court in Seattle issued a Temporary Restraining Order preventing Kentlake High School administrators from suspending Emmett.

"The court recognized that school officials do not have authority to punish students for exercising their freedom of speech outside of school. School administrators need to learn that they can't discipline students who create satires on the Internet," said Aaron Caplan, ACLU Staff Attorney who represented the student.

Emmett is a college-bound senior and a co-captain of the Kentlake High School basketball team. On the weekend of February 12 and 13, Nick and a friend posted their own site on the Internet, using the Emmett family computer and AOL account. Nick's father helped set up the graphics. Titled the "Unofficial Kentlake High Home Page," the site was intended as a light-hearted vehicle to promote discussion among the King County school's students. Nick posted compliments to the school's administration, and the home page included the disclaimer,

"This website is meant for entertainment purposes only."

At a friend's suggestion, Emmett added a fake obituary to the friend's memory; the idea came, in part, from a creative writing class in which students had been assigned to write mock obituaries. This and another obituary written in jest (with the student's permission) proved so popular that other students began posting requests for parody death notices about themselves to be written. As a humorous touch, a feature was added to the Web site enabling people to vote for the next fake obituary. At school Emmett received praise for the Web site from students and teachers alike.

After a misleading television news report aired which suggested that the site had a "hit list," Emmett and his co-creator closed the site. Two days later, Kentlake officials imposed a five-day suspension, causing him to miss a basketball playoff game. He and his parents enlisted the ACLU's help to contest the suspension in federal court.

"I went to court to fight for my rights because I don't think administrators should be able to make unfair punishments. I care about school and want to go to class," Emmett said.

On February 23, Judge Coughenour stopped the school district from enforcing the suspension. In his ruling, Judge Coughenour said: "Although the intended audience was undoubtedly connected to Kentlake High School, the speech was entirely outside of the school's supervision or control." Judge Coughenour cited the Ninth Circuit Court of Appeal's ruling in a 1988 ACLU-WA case (Burch v. Barker), which held that student distribution of non-school-sponsored material cannot be prohibited "on the basis of undifferentiated fears of possible disturbances or embarrassment to school officials."

The judge noted that the school district presented "no evidence that the mock obituaries and voting were intended to threaten anyone, did actually threaten anyone, or manifested any violent tendencies whatsover."

Freedom of Speech is freedom to
_____

Freedom of Speech is freedom of
_____

Freedom of Speech is freedom from
_____

BOUNDARIES
Societal Freedom and Individual Freedom Intersect

Most aspects of freedom in a society are about the intersection between the freedom of the individual and the freedom of the community. Often this intersection has achieved a quiet balance in which the right of the individual to have freedom is not unduly intruded upon by the right of society to protect itself. And most times society is not harmed by the desire to protect the freedom of the individual. There are still area where this balance has not been accomplished. There are societies where an individual's physical freedom is violated. There are areas of freedom where the balance between the freedom of the individual and the freedom of the society has not been achieved. This section will explore two examples of these tensions.

FREEDOM OF PRIVACY

When you walk up to a check-out line at the supermarket you are assailed by the gossip papers with their raging headlines, "Famous Actress Undergoes Plastic Surgery, See Page Five" or "Actor Caught Cheating on His Wife With Her Sister, See Page Three." Often the exciting headline is really misleading, the article just another in a long list of nonsense facts about a famous person. Other times there are photos accompanying the article, making it clear that the individual's private life is being invaded. For members of Hollywood the price of success has been the sacrifice of privacy. These individuals are not the only ones in our community who lost their right to privacy.

On the other extreme are individuals who are arrested, who also lose their right to privacy during their period as accused and convicted members of society. When an individual is arrested their personal affairs become public interest. They are branded with a criminal record that follows them for life. This loss of privacy is justified in the interests of protecting society.

Freedom to Conceal the Past

וְאִם־אָמֹר יֹאמַר הָעֶבֶד אָהַבְתִּי אֶת־אֲדֹנִי אֶת־אִשְׁתִּי
וְאֶת־בָּנָי לֹא אֵצֵא חָפְשִׁי׃ וְהִגִּישׁוֹ אֲדֹנָיו אֶל־הָאֱלֹהִים
וְהִגִּישׁוֹ אֶל־הַדֶּלֶת אוֹ אֶל־הַמְּזוּזָה וְרָצַע אֲדֹנָיו אֶת־אָזְנוֹ
בַּמַּרְצֵעַ וַעֲבָדוֹ לְעֹלָם׃

"But if the slave declares, 'I love my master and my wife and children; I do not wish to be freed,' his master shall take him before God. He shall be brought to the door or the doorpost, and his master shall pierce his ear with an awl; and he shall then remain a slave for life." (Exodus 21:5-6)

How could this be an example of Judaism trying to protect one's right to privacy?

Jewish law limits slavery and its permissibility in the ancient community. Slavery was a financial agreement that replaced the repayment of loans and other debts that an individual might have incurred. Despite the permissibility of slavery, legislation was imposed so that no individual could chose slavery as a way of life. The idea behind the above verse was that no individual would want to permanently be identified as one who chose slavery. The inability to conceal one's past was viewed as a strong deterrent from choosing slavery as a way of life.

וְאָהַבְתָּ לְרֵעֲךָ כָּמוֹךָ

"You shall love your neighbor as yourself" Rabbi Akiva said: this is the greatest precept in the Torah. *(Shabbat 31a)*

How does Rabbi Akiva's statement shed light on our freedom to privacy?

_____
_____
_____

This verse has always been interpreted to mean that you should never wish upon someone else what you would not wish upon yourself. If you treat all others in the same manner that you wish to be treated, then the world will contain a nicer range of behavior. We might also generalize that just as you would not want others to know your business, so too based on this precept, you would protect other people's right to privacy.

Ben Azzai said: "this is the book of chronologies… in the form of Adonai he created him…", this is a greater precept than that. For one should not say: because I have been humiliated, let my friend be humiliated with me, because I have been cursed, let my friend be cursed with me.

What is the difference between the opinion of Rabbi Akiva and the opinion of Ben Azzai about the 'greatest precept' of the Torah?

_____
_____
_____

The greatest precept according to Ben Azzai is recalling at all times that all are created in the image of God. This should serve as a deterrent for humiliating or bad-mouthing fellow beings. Rabbi Akiva theorized that we should each behave towards the other as we would wish to be treated, while Ben Azzai hopes that we recall that each of us is created in God's image as a deterrent for mistreating other people. Although the motivation for each is different, the end result is respecting people, their behavior, and their privacy.

Rabbi Tanhuma said: if you do that, know who you are humiliating, 'in the image of Adonai he created human.'

(Yerushalmi Talmud, Nedarim 9:4)

What does Rabbi Tanhuma add to our understanding of how to treat others?

_____

_____

_____

Our motivation according to Rabbi Tanhuma should be the recollection that when we hurt another being, when we humiliate another being, we are in fact harming God. If one exploit's another person's past, or violates their privacy, then it is God who is being violated.

In the case of a criminal, we think that we are protecting ourselves, and our community by tracking these individuals, by maintaining tabs on them. It is possible that these sources shed a different light on this behavior. By creating permanent records we might be violating the precept of respecting others as we wish to be respected. We might in fact be violating God's will by not treating even criminals with decorum and respect worthy of a creation of God. These are difficult questions, not resolved by these texts.

Freedom to be forgiven and privacy protected

It is arguable that we should have different standards for criminals because they have hurt our community. However, inherent in Judaism is the idea of forgiveness. Every year as part of the Jewish calendar all Jews have an opportunity for repentence. This concept of *tshuva*, in particular as taught by Rambam, might be another vehicle for arguing for the freedom of an individual to privacy. Rambam teaches us in *Hilkhot Tshuva* 2:2, of six stages of *tshuva* that an individual must undergo.

1) Recognition of the action as being wrong.

2) Renunciation of the wrong act, by creating distance from circumstances that would lead to this act.

3) Confession by actually stating that this was wrong to do. Stating aloud the wrongdoing is a demonstration of an awareness that this act was wrong.

4) Apologizing to God or to the person or persons who were wronged.

5) Restitution through whatever means necessary to compensate for the act.

6) Commitment that this act will never be repeated.

אי זו היא תשובה גמורה, זה שבא לידו דבר שעבר בו ואפשר
בידו לעשותו ופירש ולא עשה מפני התשובה, לא מיראה ולא
מכשלון כח,

And what is considered complete *tshuva*? It is when the opportunity arises to commit the same act again, and the person could do this act, and chooses to withdraw and not do it, and the motive is the tshuva, not fear or cowardice.

(Rambam, Hilkhot Tshuva 2:1)

EXERCISE: Freedom to Forgive and Be Forgiven

Write down a situation where you committed an act for which you should ask for tshuva:

_____

Identify all the different actions you would need to take, and who you would have to involve in order to go through all six stages of tshuva. In each stage, reflect on how you think you will (or did) feel completing this stage:

1 _____

_____

2 _____

_____

3 _____

_____

4 _____

_____

5 _____

_____

6 _____

_____

It is not clear if it is possible to preserve the opportunity for complete *tshuva* under all circumstances. How does a society allow each individual an opportunity of complete *tshuva*, while still protecting the other members of that society? Should we afford criminals a chance for total *tshuva* from their crimes, even if that entails concealing their past behavior from the community, an act which might put that community at undo risk?

Freedom to Forget

יַחֵלֹא־תִקֹּם וְלֹא־תִטֹּ֖ר
אֶת־בְּנֵ֣י עַמֶּ֔ךָ וְאָהַבְתָּ֥ לְרֵעֲךָ֖ כָּמ֑וֹךָ אֲנִ֖י יְהֹוָֽה׃

You shall not take vengeance or bear a grudge against your country-man. Love your fellow as yourself; I am Adonai. *(Leviticus 19:18)*

Why do you think that not bearing a grudge against someone, and loving another as you love yourself are taught in the same verse?

_____

_____

_____

It is very difficult to be forgiving. It is more difficult to forgive and forget. While we might accept an apology, being willing to reenter into a relationship with that individual is often more challenging.

Rashi provides a classic example of how humans bear grudges against one another: "When your neighbor comes to you and asks to borrow your hoe, and you say no. The next day he comes to you again and asks you to borrow your hoe, and you say no. When he asks you why day after day you refuse him, you respond, 'just as you wouldn't lend me your axe when I needed one last year, so too this year I will not lend you the hoe that you need.'"

Think of times when you have held a grudge against another person. What were the circumstances? Do you still hold the grudge? If so, what's preventing you from letting go?

(ג) הוא היה אומר אל תהי בז לכל אדם.
ואל תהי מפליג לכל דבר. שאין לך אדם
שאין לו שעה ואין לך דבר שאין לו מקום:

This was another favorite teaching of his (Ben Zoma): Do not disdain any person; do not underrate the importance of anything, for there is no person who does not have his hour, and there is no thing without its place in the sun. *(Pirkei Avot 4:3)*

What does Ben Zoma teach us about protecting the freedom to privacy of an individual or a community?

_____

_____

_____

In this source again we are challenged to forgive people the sins of their past and move into the future without casting judgment on their behavior. Each event in life falls into a particular place. Each person had good moments and bad moments. This brings to mind the idea that we should love others as we love ourselves. Knowing that we could each slip, we hope to treat others with the forgiving respect that we could only hope for ourselves. We can only hope for the freedom to have our past forgiven and forgotten as we try to create our futures.

COMMUNAL FREEDOMS

לֹא תַעֲמֹד עַל־דַּם רֵעֶךָ אֲנִי יְהֹוָה:

Do not stand idly by the blood of your fellow. *(Leviticus 19:16)*

What does it mean to 'stand by the blood of your fellow'?

_____

_____

_____

Defending your community is mandated by this verse. If you see another person being threatened in any way, you are commanded by this verse to take action. Human instinct often entails running for cover, or turning our backs, because what we can't see obviously can't be happening. This verse reminds us that we all have responsibility for the well being of our fellow humans. We do not live life in isolation of others, and part of communal behavior entails communal protection.

> One who is aware of a non-Jew or thief that comes against his friend and can appease him (the aggressor) on behalf of his friend and remove what he has against him but does not appease him, has transgressed 'do not stand idly by the blood of your neighbor'.
>
> *(Shulkhan Arukh, Hoshen Mishpat, 426)*

What are different ways of 'appeasing' an aggressor to avoid further harm to your friend?

_____

_____

_____

We are not only commanded to get involved in protecting our neighbor, we must actively prevent the aggressor from harming our friend. If we know something about a person that could potentially be harmful to our community we cannot forgive and forget; we must protect our neighbor by removing this obstacle from the community.

The freedom of privacy of the aggressor is not in the interest of this source. Protection of communal society is primary, taking an active stand that avoids harm for your neighbor. That would imply that a criminal who has already harmed society, has lost the right to freedom of privacy in order to allow the community to protect themselves from potential future harm. This might also teach us that even compete *tshuva* cannot erase actions of our past.

One area of concern in the tension between the freedom to privacy and the freedom of a community to protect itself comes from the advent of increased precision in the realm of medicine, allowing us to pinpoint an individual suspect based on the DNA markers. Furthermore, science is providing better methodology for identifying that DNA from minuscule samples. This has led to a tension between technology and privacy.

Those who argue in favor of increased DNA testing and record keeping see the DNA as an extension of one's social security number. This argument attempts to see these markers as one more way that society has to protect itself from those who choose to abuse the rules and regulations of the community.

Those who argue against DNA recording for police records argue that this is an intense invasion of one's privacy. The argument is that one should not be tracked worldwide because of one arrest. Furthermore, the argument continues, this methodology does not allow individuals to ever pay back the debt to society, to be rehabilitated, and then return to their basic civil rights. Such a permanent branding implies that one mistake will always follow individuals even after they have paid their debt. That is contrary to the system society has established for punishment of transgressions.

"Everything that is really great and inspiring is created by the individual who can labor in freedom"
(Albert Einstein, Out of My Later Years)

Think About This:

At age 18, a young man was accused of raping a woman in their college dorm. This young man was arrested, charged and found guilty of this violent act. After serving his sentence, the young man, with help from his parents, sought out counseling for his problems. He learned about himself, how his alcohol abuse in school and his inability to deal with his anger was expressed in this act of rape. After many years of hard work this man found himself able to rebuild his life, and was grateful to be one of the lucky ones who could find help for his problems. He also tracked down the woman he had hurt, and asked her forgiveness, promising her that he would never rape another person. Eventually this man married and had children. One day his daughter came home from high school very disturbed; it seems a classmate of hers, a good friend, had been raped the previous evening. That evening the police showed up at their door to arrest this man. His DNA was on record from his previous charged rape, and showed similar patterns to the DNA from this rape. The man could not prove that he had been one his way home from work, and did not detour and rape this young girl. His family, who did not know about his criminal history, was horrified and alienated from the community. The man continued to protest his arrest, proclaiming his innocence despite the DNA match. Only months later, after another rape in the community, was the man believed. When the rapist was arrested, it was determined that the two men shared an ethnic legacy leading their DNA to appear similar in some testing situations. By then, the damage to this man's life had already been done, damage that would never have occurred if police were not allowed to maintain long term files of people's DNA.

Do you think that the police should keep DNA files? Should there be a statute of limitations on the keeping of such files? How would you apply our Jewish sources to this situation?

_____

_____

_____

_____

Freedom of Privacy is freedom to
_____

Freedom of Privacy is freedom of
_____

Freedom of Privacy is freedom from
_____

A Call to Action—DNA Databases Hold More Dangers Than Meet the Eye

For Immediate Release

WASHINGTON — The American Civil Liberties Union today urged members of Congress to open their eyes to the unseen dangers presented by the government's zeal to create a federal database of DNA from people suspected of violating the law.

"While DNA databases may be useful to identify criminals, I am skeptical that we will ward off the temptation to expand their use," said Barry Steinhardt, Associate Director of the ACLU. "In the last ten years alone we have gone from collecting DNA only from convicted sex offenders to now including people who have been arrested but never convicted of a crime.

"There have even been proposals to store newborns' DNA for future use by law enforcement," Steinhardt added. "Although we have already entered the realm of the 'Brave New World,' it is not too late to turn back." Steinhardt's comments came in testimony before the House Judiciary Committee's Subcommittee on Crime, which is considering three different proposals to establish rules and funding for CODIS, the federal DNA database.

The ACLU urged the committee to ensure that any proposal it adopts include measures to guarantee that only persons convicted of serious violent felonies have their DNA entered into CODIS (the Combined Offender DNA Index System), that criminal defendants have access to DNA testing to establish their innocence and that the government destroy the physical sample used to provide DNA.

"While the FBI would like us to believe that the samples will never be used for anything besides catching criminals, the sad truth is that unless the samples are destroyed at some point they will be used improperly," Steinhardt said.

The Department of Defense, for example, has collected about three million samples from service personnel, purportedly to identify remains of a soldier killed on duty. Yet it not only keeps those samples long after the individual has left the military, it refuses to write rules denying third parties access to the records.

"Proponents of DNA databases argue that they can be used to prove someone's innocence just as easily as guilt. Sadly this does not hold true in the numerous states that refuse to allow people convicted of crimes access to DNA testing that might exonerate them," Steinhardt said. "It is only fair that criminal defendants be given the opportunity to use DNA technology that was not previously available."

EVOLVING FREEDOMS

In every community freedom is not an absolute guarantee. Freedom is a state of being that individuals and communities constantly strive to improve. There are particular groups in modern society that have suffered from discrimination which has resulted in limitations on their individual and communal freedom. This section will explore the evolution of these freedoms in modernity.

RACIAL FREEDOM

ברוך אתה יהוה אלהינו מלך העולם שעשני בן- (בת-)חורין

Praised are You Adonai our God, who rules the universe, making me free. *(Preliminary Prayers)*

What does it mean to thank God each day for being free?

_____
_____
_____

Do you feel free enough now to recite this blessing?

_____

_____

_____

If you were imprisoned do you think you would still recite this particular bracha as part of your daily prayer? Why or why not?

_____

_____

_____

What freedom(s) is this bracha about?

_____

_____

_____

Although the freedom referred to in this blessing is all encompassing, it is clear from the extensive list of physical attributes that follows, that the implication is first and foremost physical freedom. Every day we are grateful for the ability to awake without chains holding us back, so that we can set out on our way. However, we are also cognizant of the fact that not all members of our society are free. When we recite this bracha we must hold in mind those individuals for whom freedom is not yet a reality. We are obligated to think of them and commanded to envision ways that we can work in our daily life towards their freedom.

What is one project you (and your community) could undertake to guarantee freedom to an individual or community that is not free?

_____

_____

_____

The Premise for Racial Freedom

ומפני שלום הבריות, שלא יאמר אדם לחברו
אבא גדול מאביך. ושלא יהו מינין אומרים, הרבה רשויות בשמים.

> For the sake of peace in the human race a single person was first created, so that no person might say to another "my ancestor is greater than your ancestor"
> _(Mishnah, Sanhedrin 4:5)_

The basic premise of this source is that there is no one superior race amongst humans. The story of creation teaches us that all humans are part of one large family, descendants of one original human. There is no room within this thought for racial superiority, or supremacy. We are all one family, and this idea will ultimately promote peace and harmony in the world we inhabit.

ולהגיד גדולתו של הקדוש ברוך הוא,
שאדם טובע כמה מטבעות בחותם
אחד - כולן דומין זה לזה, ומלך מלכי המלכים הקדוש ברוך הוא טבע
כל אדם בחותמו של אדם הראשון - ואין אחד מהן דומה לחבירו.
לפיכך כל אחד ואחד חייב לומר: בשבילי נברא העולם.

The greatness of God is infinite, for while with one die man impresses many coins and all are exactly alike, the King of Kings with one die impresses the image of humanity on all people, and yet not one is like another. Thus it is that every one should say, 'for me the universe was created'. *(Babylonian Talmud, Sanhedrin 37a)*

What is the implication of being able to say that 'for me the universe was created'?

_____

_____

The universe was created for each and every human being to enjoy. To enable this enjoyment each individual must experience freedom in the universe. Racial equity is one of the manners of experiencing this ownership in the world. The text does not teach us that the universe was created for men, the text is clear in its universality. Our pursuit of justice, mandated upon us as Jews, must include a pursuit of racial equity, mandated upon us because we are created by God, in the image of God.

ואמר רבא בר מחסיא אמר רב חמא בר גוריא אמר רב: לעולם
אל ישנה אדם בנו בין הבנים, שבשביל משקל שני סלעים מילת
שנתן יעקב ליוסף יותר משאר בניו - נתקנאו בו אחיו, ונתגלגל
הדבר וירדו אבותינו למצרים

Said Rava bar Mahsiah, said Rav Hama bar Guryah, said Rav: A person should never single out one son over the others, for on account of one tunic that Jacob gave Joseph over the other brothers were they jealous of him, and the saga unfolded and our ancestors ended up down in Egypt. *(Babylonian Talmud, Shabbat 10b)*

How would you understand the prohibition to single out one son?

_____

_____

This classic understanding of the story of Joseph explains basic human nature. More than a story about family relations, this is a story about human relations. When one child is favored, when one race, gender or religion is favored, the jealousy can spawn an unfolding of events that is detrimental to everyone. The text is very straightforward in assigning the blame. Neither Joseph nor his brothers are held accountable, it is the intentions of Jacob that are reprehensible. If this is true in a familial relationship, how much more so can we hold accountable our government, our policy makers, our leaders? It is not enough to believe that we are all one family, we must be sure that it is a truth that is followed in all rules and legislation.

Struggles for Continued Racial Freedom

תנו רבנן: פעם אחת גזרה מלכות הרשעה שלא יעסקו ישראל בתורה,
בא פפוס בן יהודה ומצאו לרבי עקיבא שהיה מקהיל קהלות ברבים
ועוסק בתורה. אמר ליה: עקיבא, אי אתה מתירא מפני מלכות? אמר
לו: אמשול לך משל, למה הדבר דומה - לשועל שהיה מהלך על גב
הנהר, וראה דגים שהיו מתקבצים ממקום למקום, אמר להם: מפני
מה אתם בורחים? אמרו לו: מפני רשתות שמביאין עלינו בני אדם.
אמר להם: רצונכם שתעלו ליבשה, ונדור אני ואתם כשם שדרו
אבותי עם אבותיכם?

The Rabbis taught: Once the wicked kingdom of decreed that Israel may not study Torah. Papus ben Yehuda came to Rabbi Akiva and found him teaching Torah. He cried out to Rabbi Akiva, asking him, "are you not afraid from the death decree of the government?" Rabbi Akiva replied with a story - This is like a fox who was passing the river, and saw the fish darting about from place to place. The fox asked them why they were so scared. The fish replied, "Don't you see the fishermen with their nets up ahead?" The fox answered the fish saying, "Why don't you come up to land, and live with me, as my ancestors lived with your ancestors?"

Should the fish join the fox on land?

_____

_____

_____

אמרו לו: אתה הוא שאומרים עליך פקח
שבחיות? לא פקח אתה, אלא טפש אתה! ומה במקום חיותנו אנו
מתיראין, במקום מיתתנו על אחת כמה וכמה!

The fish answered with astonishment, "And we thought that you were the one who was considered the clever one. If we are in danger here, in our homes, how much more dangerous would it be for us to go live with a fox?!" *(Babylonian Talmud, Brachot 61b)*

How do you understand the answer of the fish to the fox?

_____

_____

_____

There are many individuals who live in fear of their lives within their natural environment. Racial freedom is about freeing individuals from the bondage of the government inequities, but it is also about freeing individuals from the fear of living in their natural environment.

Who is the fox in this allegory?

Who are the fishermen in this story?

Who is the racist—the fox or the fishermen?

Whom should the fish fear most?

Can you understand someone else's captivity, someone else's pain?

Can You See It My Way?

What is the greater threat to racial equality in our communities today? Is the fear about explicit racism or is the fear compliance, bondage's within our natural living environments? Jewish text is extremely sensitive in its understanding of the difficulties of social change. Although we are commanded to pursue justice, there is a recognition that one must not rely on good nature in order to effect change. Change can only come when there is legislative support. Furthermore, as this poignant *midrash* reads, one might not always be able to recognize where justice is not happening.

> *The caged bird says: you see my food, but you do not see my captivity.*
>
> (Kohelet Rabbah 11)

Illustrate the experience of the caged bird from the perspective of one who sees the food, the comforts tended to, for the bird:

_____
_____
_____

Illustrate the experience of the caged bird from the perspective of the bird who feels the captivity:

_____
_____
_____

How do you live in 'bondage' to your natural environment? What is the experience of growing up Jewish in your community? What is expected of you as your grow?

It is interesting to observe how our lives often reflect the opportunities offered us when growing up. A community that has an interest in soccer will often have many children involved in soccer teams. A community that resides by the ocean will often have more swimmers, while a community in a mountain snow area will have many more skiers.

Name three of the interests that a Jewish community offers its children in the natural environment of a Jewish community:

_____
_____
_____

How does this compare with what you know about the experiences of African Americans in our societies?

_____
_____
_____

Abraham Joshua Heschel on Racial Freedom

In 1963 Rabbi Abraham Joshua Heschel delivered the keynote address to the National Conference on Religion and Race. Following this conference, many clergy became involved in the fight for civil rights, for the elimination of discrimination in public places. In 1965 Heschel marched alongside Martin Luther King Jr., in Selma, in a protest march for voting rights for blacks. Of this

Photo courtesy The Heschel School, NY, NY.

march Heschel is known to have said, "In Selma I prayed with my feet." To Heschel the fight for civil liberties was a religious imperative.

Abraham Joshua Heschel was a brilliant and forceful rabbi and philosopher who found within Judaism the mandate to speak out with great urgency on issues of social justice. It was Heschel who first brought the plight of Soviet Jewry to the attention of the American community in 1962, who worked closely with Pope John XXIII to reformulate the Catholic teachings on Jews and Judaism, who helped inspire President Kennedy to convene conferences on Aging and on Children. Perhaps the most heroic act of his career was commited when he walked arm-in-arm with Dr. Martin Luther King, JR. in a civil rights demonstration in Selma, Alabama- a striking figure with a mane of white hair, becoming a symbol of Jewish activism for generations. Professor Heschel combine a lifelong devotion to scholarship with a passion for social justice which often lead him to take contraversial moral standards.

> The decisive event in the story of the Exodus of the children of Israel from Egypt was the crossing of the Red Sea.... It was a moment of supreme spiritual exaltation, of sublime joy, and found no water.... And they murmured against Moses, saying 'what shall we drink?" What a comedown! Only three days earlier they had reached the highest peak of prophetic and spiritual exaltation, and now they complain about such a prosaic and unspiritual item as water.

> The Negroes of America behave just like the Children of Israel. Only in 1963 they experienced the miracle of having turned the tide of history..... (the March to Washington) Now, only a few months later they have the audacity to murmur, "We want adequate education, decent housing, proper employment..." ....That demand for housing... seems to trite, so drab, so banal, so devoid of magnificence. (But) the teaching of Judaism is the theology of the common dead. God is concerned with everydayness, with the trivalities of life.

> *(Heschel, The Insecurity of Freedom)*

Heschel utilizes the story of the Exodus as his midrash on civil liberties, on racial freedom. When the Jews left Epypt, rather than celebrate their liberation, they complained about all that they were missing. In this mocking quote he demonstrates that it is a sacred task to be concerned not only with the larger question of legislative equality, but also with the seemingly trivial details.

Heschel reminds us all that oppression has been an integral part of the Jewish experience. Often people attempt to draw an association between the Jewish experience leaving the slavery of Egypt and the Black experience of being freed in America.

> *When Israel was in Egypt land,*
> *Let My People Go!*
>
> *They worked so hard, they could not stand,*
> *Let My People Go!*
>
> *Go down Moses, way down to Egypt land,*
> *tell old Pharaoh, Let My People Go!*
>
> *(Black Spiritual)*

This spiritual was sung on plantations across the South during the years of Black slavery in America. Today many of the Jewish community recognize it from our own Passover seder, where the song has been integrated into the telling of the Passover story. This sharing of tradition, role models and lessons has a part in creating an illusion of common heritage between two nations who were oppressed. However, it is incumbent upon us as Jews to recognize where the similarities end.

How do you feel knowing that the black slaves in the United States may have read the Biblical story of the slavery in Egypt and its redemption as inspirational to their personal journeys?

_____

_____

_____

How can we, as Jews of the North American continent at the start of the new millennium, to understand the experience of slavery?

_____

_____

_____

When you leave Egypt, any Egypt, do not stop to think, "But how will I earn a living out there?" One who stops to make provisions for the way will never get out of Egypt. (Rav Nachman Ben Simcha of Bratzlav)

"Who is to be regarded as free? Free is not always one whose actions are dominated by one's own will, since the will is not an ultimate and isolated entity but rather determined in its motivations by forces which are beyond its control. Nor is one free who is what one wants to be, since what a person wants to be is obviously determined by factors outside the person. Is one who does good for its own sake to be considered free? But how is it possible to do good for its own sake?

Humans live in bondage to their natural environment, to society, and to one's own 'character'; one is enslaved to needs, interests, and selfish desires. Yet to be free means to transcend nature, society, 'character', needs, interests, desires. How then is freedom conceivable?

The reality of freedom, of the ability to think, to will, or to make decisions beyond physiological and psychological causation is only conceivable if we assume that human life embraces both process and event. If man is treated as a process, if his future determinations are regarded as calculable of expressing himself in events beyond his being involved in the natural process of living."

(Heschel, Between God and Man)

"You can't separate peace from freedom because no one can be at peace unless he has his freedom" (Malcom X, Speech to the Militant Labor Forum, NYC, January 7, 1965)

What does Heschel mean when he writes that freedom is determined by 'factors outside the person'? Name three factors that Heschel might be referring to:

_____

_____

_____

Racial equity implies not only that everyone has equal rights, but also equal opportunities. What happens when a person is raised in a community that does not provide the same resources as a more affluent community might, such as computer services in an comfortable library, or quality books and desks in the schools? Racial equity implies that any person can walk down the street, go through an airport, or shop in a department store, without concern of being stopped simply because of the color of his or her skin.

Think About This:

Recently your town has experienced an upswing in car-jackings. The thefts have occurred in the local parking lots of the malls. In most cases, the perpetrator has approached the driver from behind while the individual was unlocking the car. The description of the thief was an African-American teenager, clean shaven and wearing a leather bomber jacket. As a result of these cases, the local police began pulling over cars driven by young black males. One night you are driving in a car with your friend from school and he is pulled over by police because he fits the profile of the perpetrator.

What do you do in response to this questioning?

_____

_____

_____

Think About This continued on next page

Think About This continued from previous page

How do you think your friend, an overachiever at the local high school who is head of the honors society, feels about being questioned by police because of his skin color?

_____

_____

How would you feel if you were questioned by police because the person was rumored to be Jewish?

_____

_____

How would you feel if everywhere you went people were suspicious of you just because you were Jewish?

_____

_____

A Call to Action—Racial Profiling

HARRISBURG, May 6 — State Rep. Harold Jams, D-Phila., wants to determine whether African-Americans, Latinos and other minorities in Pennsylvania are being pulled over for routine traffic stops simply because of their race. "It is a sad reality in our sophisticated world that a race of people seems to be scrutinized with suspicion in the eyes of justice," said James, chairman of the Pennsylvania Legislative Black Caucus.

At a Capitol news conference, James, PLBC members and other House members unveiled legislation that would require the state Attorney General's Office to determine the racial breakdown for routine traffic stops by law enforcement officers in Pennsylvania.

The breakdown would comprise the number of people stopped, their race and age, the traffic infraction which led to the stop, whether there was a search and the reason behind it, and whether there were any warnings, traffic citations or arrests. "The fact that we don't know how many people are being stopped or how many law enforcement officers are engaging in racial profiling is a serious problem," James said.

Figures from the U.S. Justice Department and the U.S. House Judiciary Committee indicate that 72 percent of drivers pulled over for routine traffic stops are African-Americans. Yet, African-Americans make up only about 14 percent of the national population. "There are too many questionable incidents regarding routine traffic stops that seem to be based on a practice of discrimination or racial profiling," James said.

Johnny Gammage, an African-American, died after being detained by police in a predominantly white Pittsburgh suburb. A federal judge in Baltimore ruled that state police target minorities for searches on Interstate 95. Black motorists stopped on Florida's turnpike by an all-white sheriff's drug squad are searched 6.5 times more than white drivers. Legal suits are pending in Rhode Island, Illinois, Maryland and North Carolina by minority motorists who claim they were pulled over simply because of their race.

In Pennsylvania, Tinicum Township in Delaware County settled a lawsuit for $220,000 in 1994 for stopping drivers on Interstate 95 near the Philadelphia International Airport because they fit a race-based drug courier profile. "Racial profiling is a real problem," said James, who represents the 186th Legislative District. "Something needs to be done to protect the respect we have for our police officers, as well as to ensure the individual rights and freedoms of every Pennsylvania citizen."

"Every citizen, regardless or race or gender, deserves equal treatment under the law," James said. "The sharp contrast in the number of African-Americans, Latinos and other minorities who are stopped for routine traffic violations is disturbing. Breaking this pattern of discrimination means breaking the silence.

http://www.pahouse.net/james/pr/186050698.htm

Racial Freedom is freedom to

_____

Racial Freedom is freedom of

_____

Racial Freedom is freedom from

_____

GENDER EQUITY

This past century has witnessed among other changes the ordination of women as Rabbis, the establishment of formal guidelines allowing professional women's sports teams, women going to the moon, and a woman candidate for Vice President of the United States. It is impossible to talk about the twentieth century without discussing gender freedom, and it is impossible to discuss freedom today without discussing gender. The onset and evolution of gender equity in our secular community has been accompanied by growing conversations and changes in our religious communities.

A Timeline of the Evolution of Egalitarianism in Conservative Judaism

1955
Aliyot
Three opinions presented to CJLS One opposed women getting *aliyot*, one asked for *aliyot* on special occasions, and one granted *aliyot* on an equal basis.

1973
Minyan
CJLS determine that women can count in a minyan on basis of *takannah* (legislative enactment). Also upheld opinion that women not be counted in minyan.

1973
Shaliach Tzibbur
Takannah on minyan interpreted to mean that women may serve as communal leaders of prayer.

1974
Witnesses
One opinion opposes women serving as witnesses for any ritual event, another opinion supporting women serving as witnesses, even for ritual moments.

1975
Aliyot
Chair of CJLS wrote to congregations that did not count women in a minyan indicating that women there could still be granted aliyot.

1977
Aliyot
One opinion that women cannot be granted Cohen or Levi aliyot, other opinion granting *aliyot* for *b'not Cohen*.

1977
Ordination
Resolution of the Rabbinical Assembly calling upon the Jewish Theological Seminary to admit women to the Rabbinical School.

1983
Shaliach Tzibbur
Paper by Rabbi Joel Roth accepted regarding ordination of women, requires a woman to have accepted upon herself hiyyuv (obligated) in order to serve as a communal leader of prayer.

1997
Minyan
Declaration of chancellor Ismar Schorsch that women at the Seminary synagogue be counted in the minyan with no need to have accepted upon themselves hiyyuv.

For many Jews in the Conservative movement the culmination of the transformation towards egalitarianism came with the ordination of women as rabbis. In 1977 then Chancellor Gerson Cohen established a commission to explore the role of women as spiritual leaders in the Conservative Movement. In 1983 the faculty of the Jewish Theological Seminary of America voted to admit women to the Rabbinical (and consequently Cantorial) School. This was followed in 1985 with the ordination of the first woman, Rabbi Amy Eilberg.

LOOK TO THE SOURCES

תנו רבנן: הכל עולין
למנין שבעה, ואפילו קטן ואפילו אשה. אבל אמרו חכמים: אשה לא
תקרא בתורה, מפני כבוד צבור.

Our Rabbis taught: all are qualified to be counted among the seven (aliyot to the Torah), even a minor, even a woman. But the Sages said that a woman should not read Torah our of respect for the congregation. *(Babylonian Talmud, Megillah 23a)*

What do you think the meaning of the phrase "respect for the congregation" teaches?

_____

_____

_____

Most individuals who have written in favor of including women in religious ritual read this passage as a primary indicator that the limitations on women's participation were social ones. The 'respect for the congregation' was viewed as a limitation that is not relevant in today's society where men and women are equal members of an integrated society. Those who oppose inclusion of women in ritual do not view equal as sameness and want to preserve the ritual distinction between the genders.

וכל מצות עשה שהזמן גרמה,
אנשים חייבין ונשים פטורות. וכל מצות עשה שלא הזמן גרמה, אחד
אנשים ואחד נשים חייבין.

And all positive time-bound commandments are incumbent upon men, but women are exempted. And all positive commandments which are not time-bound, both men and women are commanded. *(Mishnah Kiddushin 1:7)*

Why would women be exempt from time-bound commandments?

_____

_____

_____

The exemption of women from time-bound positive commandments is a core distinction between those who embrace egalitarianism and those who do not in the Conservative movement. Should it be assumed that women, because of their social roles as mother or wide, be exempt from time bound commandments so that they will not sin when they put family ahead of ritual? Or in modern day, when gender roles in the home may have changed, when responsibilities are shared, should both partners of a marriage be equally commanded (or equally exempt) from these positive time bound commandments?

Rabbi Yitzhak HaLevi has rendered a decision that women are not to be prevented from reciting the blessings on sukkah and lulav. For the contention that women are exempt from time bound positive commandments is meant only to indicate that they are not obligated. But if they wish to bring themselves under the yoke of the mitzvot, they are entitled to do so, and should not be prevented.

(Responsa of Rashi)

What is the implication of women accepting the yoke of mitzvot on the role of women in Judaism?

_____

_____

_____

Two Conservative Rabbis on Gender Equity in Jewish Ritual

The Rabbis formulated the legal dictum that women are exempt from mitzvot which are to be performed at specific times. They derived this principle as follows:

1. women are exempt from the study of Torah
2. from the juxtaposition of the commandment for men to study Torah and to put on Tfillin, the Rabbis deduce that women are exempt from putting on Tfillin.
3. the mitzvah of putting on Tfillin is a time bound positive mitzvah
4. since women are exempt from this time bound mitzvah, they are exempt from all time bound mitzvot

However, the Abudraham suggests: The reason why women are exempt from time bound positive mitzvot is because '*ha-isha medhabedet le-baalah*', the woman is bound to do her husband's bidding. If she had to fulfill time bound positive mitzvot, a time would come when she couldn't do her husband's bidding and would incur the displeasure of her husband. But if she did his bidding, she would abandon a mitzvah and would incur her Creator's displeasure. That kind of rigid separation of the sexes fixed in the past by custom or by *halakha* today reflects the practice of a diminishing minority of Jews. To oppose change merely because it is change is to ask humankind to stop thinking, inventing and aspiring. And the Jewish people are part of humanity. The present status of women in American society has its theological roots in the biblically grounded conceptions of the dignity and sacredness of the individual. It is therefore altogether congenial to our biblically rooted tradition and can be integrated in the *Halakha* in accordance with halakhically valid principles.

(Exerpted from Rabbi Simon Greenberg, "The Question of the Ordination of Women as Rabbis by the Jewish Theological Seminary of America")

Rabbi Simon Greenberg (1901-1993) was former Provost of the Jewish Theological Seminary, past Executive Director of the United Synagogue, one of the founders of USY, President and moving force behind the founding of the University of Judaism in Los Angeles, Vice-Chancellor of the Seminary, and former President of the Rabbinical Assembly. One of Conservative Judaism's most articulate and perservering spokesperson, he stressed the centrality of the Jewish people, the importance of Zionism, the religious character of American civilization, and the importance of Hebrew in Jewish education.

Dorff,
— Conservative Judaism

Compare the sources quoted by Rabbi Greenberg to the sources studied on the previous pages:

How would the arguments presented by Rabbi Greenberg be defended or negated by these sources?

_____

_____

_____

How does Rabbi Greenberg answer those who would not grant gender equity in Jewish ritual?

_____

_____

_____

Dr. Joel Roth is Louis Finkelstein Professor of Jewish Thought and Halakha at the Jewish Theological Seminary. An expert in halakha, he was appointed to the Committee on Jewish Law and Standards of the Rabbinical Assembly in 1978 and served as its chairman for eight years.

1. May women perform those mitzvot from which they are exempt and may they recite the appropriate blessings?
2. If women may observe mitzvot from which they are exempt, is their observance of these mitzvot governed by the same rules as is the observance of these mitzvot by men.
3. Can the voluntary observance of a mitzvah ever become in some religious sense obligatory?
4. If it can, can that self-imposed obligation have the same legal status as the obligation of men?

Women may be counted in a minyan or serve as a leader of communal prayer, only when they have accepted upon themselves the voluntary obligation to pray as required in halakha, and affirm that failure to comply with the obligation is sin. Then they may be counted in a minyan, serve as agent for others, and become ritual leaders of Jewish communities.

(Exerpted from Rabbi Joel Roth, "The Ordination of Women as Rabbis")

Compare the sources quoted by Rabbi Roth to the sources studied on the previous pages:

How would the arguments presented by Rabbi Roth be defended or negated by these sources?

_____

_____

_____

How does Rabbi Roth answer those who would not grant gender equity in Jewish Ritual?

_____

_____

_____

Rabbi Greenberg and Rabbi Roth come to the same conclusion that women can be ordained as rabbis, and that all women can serve as leaders of Jewish ritual in their communities. Despite this agreement, the two differ in the manner by which they reach their conclusion. The text that they refer to is similar, they are both concerned with the question of time bound positive commandments, but their investigation and treatment of the text lead them down varying paths.

Freedom for the Minority?

The position papers on the ordination of women as rabbis reflect the ways in which some members of the Conservative movement approach halakha, and the ways in which they approach the question of gender freedom in Judaism. The ordination of women as rabbis was perceived by some to be the culmination of gender equity in Judaism. For those who have opposed the ordination of women as rabbis, and the involvement of women in Jewish ritual, this process has brought them to ask how they can find their freedom within the Conservative movement.

Rabbi Ismar Schorsch, Chancellor of the Jewish Theological Seminary, has recently spoken of egalitarian Judaism being the future of Conservative movement. This position questions what happens to the freedom of those individuals who hold halakhic positions that are not egalitarian.

What do you think the future of gender freedom in Jewish ritual in the Conservative movement should be?

_____
_____
_____
_____
_____
_____

What is the implication of your position on egalitarianism towards other people's freedoms to hold a different halakhic position?

_____
_____
_____

One of the biggest challenges in a movement that is constantly changing and evolving, is the ability to embrace and grant freedom to those who hold differing views. How should Conservative Judaism grant freedom for those who hold a different halakhic position than you?

_____
_____
_____
_____
_____

Think About This:

The position of Senior Cantor in your synagogue has opened, and the committee has been formed to search for a new cantor. As the president of your USY chapter you have been invited to represent the youth population of the synagogue on this committee. Your synagogue is egalitarian and has been for many years. You know that there has been at least one woman president of the executive board, although most members of the board are men. It has never occurred to you that there would be a gender question introduced to the selection of a new cantor. However, the committee is reviewing five applicants, two of whom are women. Some members of the committee feel there is no point in even interviewing the women, because it would not be right to 'impose' a woman cantor on the community as their Senior Cantor. Other members of the committee are willing to interview these women, but aren't sure if the women are 'suitable' to be the Senior Cantor at a large congregation.

How do you respond to these suggestions?

_____

_____

_____

Do you think that it is legitimate to not interview a cantor because she would not be acceptable to the community?

_____

_____

_____

Do you think that there is legitimate space to say that there are people 'not ready' for a woman to be their cantor?

_____

_____

_____

Do you think this is a case of a 'glass ceiling' within religion?

_____

_____

_____

Egalitarianism is freedom to

_____

Egalitarianism is freedom of

_____

Egalitarianism is freedom from

_____

CIVIC EQUALITY FOR HOMOSEXUALS

Freedom for gays and lesbians in our communities is an issue that confronts us as a Conservative movement. It is a question of freedom that we ponder now, but leave its resolution for future generations. It is an issue that engages the Conservative movement in controversy beyond the scope of this book. It would be negligent to omit this topic from our list of freedom issues, but it would be irresponsible to imagine that we will reach resolution within the confines of space and time that a book such as this provides. This issue is explored in greater depth in the Rabbinic letter, "This is My Beloved, This is My Friend," under the auspices of The Commission on Human Sexuality of The Rabbinical Assembly, and authored by Rabbi Elliot Dorff.

The United Synagogue of Conservative Judaism accepted a resolution affirming that all humans are created in the image of the divine. This resolution further restated our sensitivity as Jews to civil prejudice and civil discrimination. It supports full civil liberties for all humans. The resolution of the United Synagogue does not address the questions of religious or ritual freedoms; these questions are in the realm of halakhic decisions that are engaged by the Committee on Jewish Law and Standards.

United Synagogue in its resolution recognizes that there have been crimes of hate, as well as pains of alienation experienced by gay and lesbian Jews and the anguish of their family and friends.

In light of these realities, the United Synagogue called upon its communities to support full civil equality for gays and lesbians. Civil liberty does not reflect religious or ritual practices of any community, but remains in the national social and political domain. Furthermore, this resolution denounces hate crimes of all forms, and hate crimes against gays and lesbians.

How does such a resolution provide freedom to _____?

_____

_____

How does such a resolution provide freedom of _____?

_____

_____

How does such a resolution provide freedom from _____?

_____

_____

Are there individuals or communities whose freedom is limited when the civil liberties of gays and lesbians are granted?

_____

_____

_____

The Power of Words

> O Lord guard my tongue from evil and my lips from speaking lies. To those who curse me may I be silent. May my soul be humble. Open my heart to your Torah and may I pursue fulfillment of your *mitzvot*.
> (Closing meditation of the *Amidah--Talmud Berakhot 16b-17a*)

Three times a day, daily, a Jew recited the *Amidah*, and concludes it with a private meditation. This meditation is *Elohai N'tzor*, O Lord guard my tongue from evil. "*Elohai N'tzor*, contains the following ideas:

    a. Life and death are in the power of the tongue
    b. Now that we've completed the *Amidah*, let us not be overcome by those who would try to stop us from improving ourselves.
    c. God should answer our prayer because God is gracious and loving.
    d. Our intellect and emotions should be open to God's teachings."*

Why is it that when you call someone or something 'stupid' you might refer to it as being 'gay'? How might usage of such language impact on the civil liberties of those who are gay and lesbian?

_____

_____

_____

Think about it:

You are a member of the cross-country track team at your high school. You are changing in the lockers when you overhear a conversation about a fellow teammate. As you stand there you realize that there is a plan to corner your teammate on his way home from school, and beat him up because he is gay. You are scared for your friend. What are you going to do? You are scared that if you speak up in the locker room these guys will attack you for defending your friend. You are concerned that if you tell a teacher you will be alienated as being a 'tattle'. How do you stand up for what is right? How do you stop a crime of hatred? How will you be part of the solution and not part of the silence? How do you preserve his freedoms?

_____

_____

_____

_____

_____

_____

_____

*Steven Brown. Higher and Higher: Making Jewish Prayer Part of Us.

Section Five: The Call to Freedom

כל ישראל ערבים זה בזה

All of Israel are responsible for one another

This precept has motivated generations of Jews to a life of action rather than compliance, to a life of creative intervention rather that submissive acceptance. We are charged in our lives to work towards tikun olam, we are charged in our lives to bring freedom to the earth and all its inhabitants.

Why do you think that the Jewish community worldwide has a responsibility to help other Jewish communities around the world?

_____

_____

_____

How do you think that the Jewish community has a responsibility to help communities in need around the world that are not Jewish?

_____

_____

_____

Many celebrations in Judaism focus on the importance of our freedom. When we pray, we are reminded that being free is a tremendously important concept in Jewish life. Nevertheless, even today, many people –Jews and non-Jews alike – are not free to choose how or where they live, and how they express their religious values and practices. Over the past fifty years, the Jewish community world wide, led by the State of Israel, has rallied in large numbers in support of the release of Jews from the Former Soviet Union, Ethiopia, and Syria.

May we feel at home with your Torah and cling to your *mitzvot*. Keep us from error, from sin and transgression. Bring us not to trial or to disgrace. Let no evil inclination control us. Keep us far from wicked people and corrupt companions. Strengthen our desire to do good deeds; teach us humility, that we may serve you. May we find grace, love, and compassion in your sight and in the sight of all who look upon us, this day and every day. Grant us a full measure of lovingkindness. Praised are You, Adonai, who bestows lovingkindness upon his people Israel.

(Siddur Sim Shalom from Berachot 60b)

There is no particular bracha that one would recite before engaging in an action to bring freedom to the world. Nonetheless, this particular blessing, recited each morning as part of *birkot hashachar*, reflects the values wrapped up in the quest to safeguard freedom in the world. We seek out the freedom to make the right choices that will heal the world and bring it peace. We seek out ways to sanctify the world we inhabit, bringing God's spirit to all that we do. It is not enough to study, it is not enough to have faith, we are sanctioned to do good deeds, to serve God by serving our communities, by serving the world we inhabit.

תנו רבנן: (ויקרא יא) והתקדשתם
והייתם קדשים - אדם מקדש עצמו מעט -מקדשין אותו הרבה,

A person who raises his level of holiness just a little will be raised by it a lot   *(Babylonian Talmud, Yoma 39a)*

This source teaches us that you should start by taking action for a single mitzvah, that you should take on a single cause. Whether you alert your government about the plight of Syrian Jews, or combat racism in your local community, you will be bringing all one step closer to freedom.

PIDYON SHEVUYIM – Freedom for those in Captivity

Pidyon Shevuyim is the *mitzvah* of redeeming captives. From the earliest centuries of our history as a nation, we have been faced with the necessity of gaining our freedom. During many historical periods, large numbers of our people were enslaved or held captive; during others, individuals were the objects of kidnapping and imprisonment for the sake of ransom. We are well aware of the problem of soldiers missing in action. During and after the Vietnam War, Jews and non-Jews alike have felt pain and sorrow for the POW's/MIA's and their families. Frequently we were able to buy our freedom and the freedom of our brothers. Sometimes, however, even money has been insufficient to redeem Jews held captive, and other means have been sought to secure their freedom.

How can we agree on a modern definition of the word 'captive' in modern terms?

_____

_____

_____

What are some situations in modern Jewish history when Jews were held captive or hostage?

_____

_____

_____

> Redeeming captives takes precedence over providing food and clothing for poor people because captives are considered to be in the category of thirsty, hungry, and naked people. They are also considered to be in danger of their lives.
>
> _(Mishneh Torah Laws of Gifts to the Poor, chapt. 8, par.10)_

Being a captive means being dependent upon the will of some power greater than the Jewish community. Captivity may also be defined by the desire of the captor to exact some payment, penalty or recognition from those who wish to save the captive. When a Jewish Community has limited funds and cannot ransom all the captives that need redeeming, there would understandably be a great deal of time that might be wasted deciding the issue. Jewish Law tries to save this valuable time by setting priorities to assure that at least someone will be saved from captivity.

Have you ever participated in a project which involved raising awareness for the release of Jews from these communities? (e.g. Rallies for Soviet Jewry, Israel's MIA's, letter writing, etc.)

Calling out for Freedom

The Jewish community has traditionally felt the need to help other Jews who were captives. Jews felt this need for a number of reasons: they believed that every Jews was responsible for other Jews. They recognized the possibility that they too might someday be captives of some regime or another—and would want their brothers to work on their behalf for their freedom. They believed that captivity ultimately would result in the loss of the lives of the captives—and Jews were willing to make great sacrifices in order to save lives—Jewish or non-Jewish.

We live in countries where many of us take our freedom for granted. In our Jewish communities, we never have to hide our shabbat candles, sneak into our synagogues or sell prayer books, kippot or t'fillin underground. Our government does not suppress our voice as a community. In fact, throughout the United States and Canada, the Jewish community is one of the most powerful voices on the political scene today.

Israel and the North American Jewish community have worked together to free massive amounts of oppressed Jews from communities in Europe, the Former Soviet Union, Ethiopia and Syria. Many of the largely populated oppressed Jewish communities around the world have already been freed and are now living in Israel and throughout the Diaspora.

The Price of Freedom

Inhabitants of a town who have raised funds to build a synagogue but see that performing another mitzvah required the money they have collected. Should they donate the money towards that mitzvah or keep the money for what it was allocated?

_____

_____

_____

What if the mitzvah was Pidyon Shevuyim?

_____

_____

_____

> Inhabitants of a town who have raised funds to build a synagogue but who see that performing another mitzvah required the money they have collected, should donate the money towards that mitzvah. If they purchased stones and beams (for building the synagogue) they should not sell them in order to perform another mitzvah except Pidyon Shevuyim. Even if they have brought the stones (to the building site) and laid their foundation, and if they have carved the beams, and prepared everything for the building, they may sell all the materials only for Pidyon Shevuyim. But if they have completed the building, they need not sell the synagogue, but must raise more money (for Pidyon Shevuyim) from the community.
>
> *Maimonides, Mishneh Torah, Laws of Gifts to the Poor, 8:11*

Being a captive means being dependent upon the will of some power greater than the Jewish community. Captivity may also be defined by the desire of the captor to exact some payment, penalty or recognition from those who wish to save the captive. When a Jewish Community has limited funds and cannot free all the captives that need redeeming, there would understandably be a great deal of time that might be wasted deciding the issue. Jewish Law tries to save this valuable time by setting priorities to assure that at least someone will be saved from captivity.

How much can you collect in ransom for a captive? Can you help them escape?

> One should not pay an exorbitant amount of money in order to redeem captives. Paying too large a sum will encourage kidnappers to continue taking captives. One should not attempt to rescue captives because this will cause the captors to treat the captives worse, and to watch them more closely.
>
> *Mishneh Torah Laws of Gifts to the Poor, chap. 8, par. 12*

Think About This:

In 1976, terrorists hijacked a plane to Entebbe, Uganda and held all Jews (many Israelis) as captives. The Israelis made a basically successful rescue: however, one rescuer, Lt. Colonel Yonaton Netanyahu and three passagers were killed: Jean-Jacques Maimon, Ida Borowicz, and Pasco Cohen. Most people would probably agree that the Israelis did the right thing, even though 4 people died in the process.

Do you agree? If not, what do you think should have happened?

_____

_____

_____

In the Spring of 1980, an American attempt to rescue its hostages in Iran failed before it every really got off the ground. A number of American servicemen were killed, and the Iranian captors separated the hostages from each other making life much harder on the hostages.

Was this rescue worth attempting even though lives were lost?

_____

_____

_____

In 1985, Israel released 1,150 Palestinian and other terrorists—including mass murders—in exchange for three Israeli soldiers who fell into terrorist hands in Lebanon in 1982.

Do think this was a fair exchange? Why or why not?

_____

_____

_____

For each captive who must be redeemed, how is the freedom of that individual important to guaranteeing the freedom of the community?

_____

_____

_____

How much do you value your freedom?
What is your freedom worth to you?
Can you put a price on the value of your freedom?
How much could your freedom be limited before you rose up in protest?

How much do you value someone else's freedom?
What is someone else's freedom worth to you?
Can you put a price on the value of their freedom?
How much could their freedom be limited before you rose up in protest?

What are you willing to do about guaranteeing these freedoms?

Call out for freedom! Go out into the world and guarantee freedom to all the inhabitants! In a society in which every individual is free, some freedom must be limited or controlled by that same society. That leaves every individual free to have a voice in how the society chooses to limit freedoms, in order to preserve the integrity of the system.

In Judaism we reenact our freedom by accepting God's call to be chosen, by accepting the obligation of Torah, of *halakka*, and living our lives within that system. We sanctify God's world by accepting responsibility for guaranteeing freedom for all humanity in this world.

A Psalm of Asaph

אמזמוֹר לְאָסָף אֱלֹהִים נִצָּב בַּעֲדַת־אֵל בְּקֶרֶב אֱלֹהִים

יִשְׁפֹּט: בְּעַד־מָתַי תִּשְׁפְּטוּ־עָוֶל וּפְנֵי רְשָׁעִים תִּשְׂאוּ־סֶלָה:

גּשִׁפְטוּ־דָל וְיָתוֹם עָנִי וָרָשׁ הַצְדִּיקוּ: דַפַּלְטוּ־דַל וְאֶבְיוֹן מִיַּד

רְשָׁעִים הַצִּילוּ: הֹלֹא יָדְעוּ | וְלֹא יָבִינוּ בַּחֲשֵׁכָה יִתְהַלָּכוּ

יִמּוֹטוּ כָּל־מוֹסְדֵי אָרֶץ: וַאֲנִי אָמַרְתִּי אֱלֹהִים אַתֶּם וּבְנֵי

עֶלְיוֹן כֻּלְּכֶם: זָאָכֵן כְּאָדָם תְּמוּתוּן וּכְאַחַד הַשָּׂרִים תִּפֹּלוּ:

חקוּמָה אֱלֹהִים שָׁפְטָה הָאָרֶץ כִּי־אַתָּה תִנְחַל בְּכָל־הַגּוֹיִם:

God rises in the court of the mighty, He pronounces judgment over judges. How long will you pervert justice? How long will you favor the wicked? Champion the weak and the orphan uphold the downtrodden and destitute; Rescue the weak and the needy; save them from the grip of the wicked. But they neither know nor understand; they wander about in darkness while the earths foundations are shaken. I thought you were God-like, children of the Most High, but you will die like mortals like any prince you will fall. Arise, O God, and judge the earth for your dominion is over all nations.

(Psalm 82, Siddur Sim Shalom, p.27)

This psalm, recited as the *Shir Shel Yom* (Psalm of the Day), every Tuesday, illustrates through the negative, the beauty of human free will. If not for our free will, we would not be able to make the choices that allow us to do evil. By describing the wrong choices that the evil make, this psalm is able to teach us what good choices are. It is because of the freedom of choice that God needs to intervene in the world and protect people.

God knows that free will is higher than any other moral precepts in the world. That is why people continue to abuse their free will, to err in their ways, and God still sits quietly, hopefully, waiting for them to use their freedom responsibly in the world.

Another person who stated so eloquently our mutual obligation as a community to guarantee freedom to all individuals was United States President John Fitzgerald Kennedy. He understood that it was possible to await intervention from a higher source. He also knew that true redemption would only come when individuals stood up and did things for themselves. And so he said in his famous inaugural address:

> "And so, my fellow Americans: Ask not what your country can do for you - ask what you can do for your country. My fellow citizens of the world: Ask not what America will do for you, but what together we can do for the freedom of man."
> *Inaugural address, January 20ᵗʰ, 1961*

In Siddur Sim Shalom there is a Talmudic reading that is studied each morning before the recitation of Kaddish D'Rabbanan. This passage illustrates how humans can use their freedom to make the good choices to do good in this world. If we do these good deeds, we are behaving "In God's Image" and bringing sanctification to this world.

לָלֶכֶת בְּכָל־דְּרָכָיו. אֵלוּ דַרְכֵי הַקָּדוֹשׁ בָּרוּךְ הוּא, שֶׁנֶּאֱמַר: יהוה יהוה אֵל רַחוּם וְחַנּוּן אֶרֶךְ אַפַּיִם וְרַב חֶסֶד וֶאֱמֶת, נוֹצֵר חֶסֶד לָאֲלָפִים נֹשֵׂא עָוֹן וָפֶשַׁע וְחַטָּאָה וְנַקֵּה.... מָה הַמָּקוֹם נִקְרָא רַחוּם וְחַנּוּן, אַף אַתָּה הֱוֵי רַחוּם וְחַנּוּן.... מָה הַקָּדוֹשׁ בָּרוּךְ הוּא נִקְרָא צַדִּיק, שֶׁנֶּאֱמַר, צַדִּיק יהוה בְּכָל־דְּרָכָיו, אַף אַתָּה הֱוֵי צַדִּיק. הַקָּדוֹשׁ בָּרוּךְ הוּא נִקְרָא חָסִיד, שֶׁנֶּאֱמַר, וְחָסִיד בְּכָל־מַעֲשָׂיו, אַף אַתָּה הֱוֵי חָסִיד.

> "To walk in all His ways" (Deuteronomy 11:22). These are the ways of the Holy One: "Gracious and compassionate, patient, abounding in kindness and faithfulness, assuring love for a thousand generations, forgiving iniquity, transgression and sin, and granting pardon..." (Exodus 34:6). This means that just as God is gracious and compassionate, you too must be gracious and compassionate. "The Adonai is righteous in all His ways and loving in all his deeds: (Psalm 145:17). As the Holy One is righteous, you too must be righteous. As the Holy One is loving, you too must be loving.
> *(Sifre Deuteronomy, Ekev, from Siddur Sim Shalom, p.19)*

What does it mean to walk in the path of God? It means exercising our freedom to do good in the world that we live in. It means embodying the meaning of being created in God's image by imitating God's love and concern for the world through our personal actions. Each action is one that we choose to do, but we must know that these choices are the moral choices, these are the choices on the path to seeking justice in the world. These are the choices that alter our lives from the mundane to the sanctified, from the meaningless to the meaningful.

Freedom in Judaism is not about an absolute experience for each individual. Freedom is about a community in which each individual is free to live, grow, and prosper. We do so because we are each created *"betzelem elohim,"* we are created in God's image. Our behavior guarantees freedom to the others living in our community. That freedom is reciprocated to each of us, and in that way we create sacred time, space and behavior. That is a free Jewish society.

Who you are as a person, who you are as a member of a community, is all dependent on your ability to embrace your freedom, to respect others freedoms and to work towards all freedoms.

> Live Judaism passionately. Whether your preference is for the prophetic legacy of social and political action; the Talmudic model of untangling the knots of logic and laying them out end to end; the philosophical, mystical, liturgical, ritual or national- learn it, do it, live it passionately. (Rabbi Nina Beth Cardin)

May you each be blessed
with your unique abilities as Jews
to bring freedom to this world in any which way you can.

Organizations, Web Sites, and Other Resources

www.mazon.org
This site is dedicated to help individuals contribute 3% of their celebrations to those in need, in an attempt to stamp out hunger and need from our communities.

www.socialaction.com
This site is a compilation of information and activism for Jews of Northern America who are seeking ways to become more socially involved in their communities.

www.workingforchange.com
This site allows individuals shopping on the world wide web to choose the charity of their choice. Each time a purchase is made on line, this site makes a charitable donation to that charity.

www.freedomforum.org
This website is home to a non-partisan international foundation dedicated to free press, free speech, and free spirit for all people

www.ajc.org/wwa/jbi
This website is the home of the Jacob Blaustein Institute for the Advancement of Human Rights. This site provide international information about human right violations, with a particular focus on rights of Jews around the world.

www.aclu.org
This site is dedicated to American Civil liberties. These liberties include freedoms of speech, religion, economics, gender and more. This site provides news updates, policy information and ideas for activism.

www.ojp.uddoj.gov/nij/dna
This commission is dedicated to making public announcements and information about the future of DNA evidence in criminal investigations in the United States.

Million Mother March
This march was organized by concerned citizens who feel that the gun lobby in Washington D.C. has overshadowed the actual issues involved with guns in our communities, including gun safety, license checks and other guidelines that might increase gun security.

www.religioustolerance.org
This site is dedicated to providing comprehensive information on social issues with a focus on the differences between religious opinions, including ethical questions and legal stands in the United States.

Acknowledgements, Works Cited and Bibliography

Artson, Bradley Shavit. (1995) *It's A Mitzvah.* New Jersey: Behrman House.

Baker, Daniel. (1992) *Power Quotes.* Detroit: Visible Ink Press.

Blecher, Arthur and Louis Zivic (Eds.) (1971) *Yesterday We Were Slaves: Today We Are Free.* New York: National Youth Commission, United Synagogue of Conservative Judaism.

Blumenthal, Jacob (Ed.) (1995) *The Abortion Controversy: Jewish Religious Rights and Responsibilities.* A United Synagogue Resolution Implementation Packet. New York: United Synagogue of Conservative Judaism.

Brawarsky, Sandee and Deborah Mark. (1998) Two Jews, Three Opinions. New York: Perigee Books.

Brown, Steven. (1988) *Higher and Higher: Making Jewish Prayer Part of Us.* New York: National Youth Commission, United Synagogue of Conservative Judaism.

Cardin, Rabbi Nina Beth. (1997) Visions of Holiness in the Everyday. National Youth Commission, United Synagogue of Conservative Judaism.

Dorff, Rabbi Elliot N. (1996) *Conservative Judaism: Out Ancestors to Our Descendants.* National Youth Commission, United Synagogue of Conservative Judaism.

Dorff, Elliot & Louis Newman. (1995) *Contemporary Jewish Ethics and Morality.* New York: Oxford University Press.

Gillman, Neil. (1993) *Conservative Judaism.* New Jersey: Behrman House.

Greenberg, Simon. (1998) *The Ordination of Women as Rabbis.* New York: The Jewish Theological Seminary of America.

Harlow, Rabbi Jules (Ed.) (1975) *Machzor for Rosh Hashanah and Yom Kippur.* New York: Rabbinical Assembly. Used with permission.

………. (1998) *Siddur Sim Shalom.* New York: Rabbinical Assembly and United Synagogue of Conservative Judaism. Used with permission.

Heschel, Abraham Joshua. (1998) *The Sabbath.* New York: Noonday Press.

………. (1966) The Insecurity of Freedom. Philadelphia: Jewish Publication Society of America.

Isaacs, Rabbi Ronald (1998) *Derech Eretz: The Path to an Ethical Life*. New York: National Youth Commission, United Synagogue of Conservative Judaism.

Kolatch, Alfred. (1996) *Great Jewish Quotations*. New York: Jonathan David Publishers.

Lewy, Altmann, and Heinemann (Eds.) (1969) *Three Jewish Philosophers*. Philadelphia: Jewish Publication Society of America.

Moline, Jack. (1987) *Jewish Leadership and Heroism*. New York: National Youth Commission, United Synagogue of Conservative Judaism.

Novick, Bernard. (1994) *In God's Image*. New York: National Youth Commission, United Synagogue of Conservative Judaism.

Steinberg, Barbara, Dara Zabb (Revised Edition) (1999) *Tzorchei Tzibbur: Community and Responsibility in the Jewish Tradition*. New York: National Youth Commission, United Synagogue of Conservative Judaism.

Thomas, Marlo. (1998) *Free To Be You and Me*. Philadelphia: Running Press.

The Oxford Dictionary of Quotations: 3rd Edition, (1980) New York: Oxford University Press.

About the Author

Rabbi Karen Gluckstern-Reiss is the Principal of Machon Beth Sholom, the religious afternoon high school at Temple Beth Sholom in Roslyn Heights, New York.

Rabbi Gluckstern-Reiss was ordained by The Jewish Theological Seminary of America in 1995. Rabbi Gluckstern-Reiss is the curriculum consultant in Rabbinics for the new middle school at Perelman Day School in Philadephia, PA.

Rabbi Gluckstern-Reiss grew up in Beer-Sheva, Israel and returned to New York for her undergraduate and Rabbinic education. She is currently a resident of Forest Hills, New York, and a member of the Forest Hills Jewish Center.

Rabbi Gluckstern-Reiss is the widow of Cantor Joshua Gluckstern-Reiss (ז"ל).